Winning Either Way

By Peter R. Garber

First Edition

Oshawa, Ontario

Winning Either Way
by Peter R. Garber

Managing Editor: Kevin Aguanno
Acquisitions Editor: Sarah Schwersenska
Copy Editor: Susan Andres
Typesetting: Peggy LeTrent
Cover Design: Troy O'Brien

Published by:
Multi-Media Publications Inc.
Box 58043, Rosslynn RPO
Oshawa, ON, Canada, L1J 8L6

http://www.mmpubs.com/

All rights reserved. No part of this book may be reproduced or transmitted in any form or by any means, electronic or mechanical, including photocopying, recording or by any information storage and retrieval system, without written permission from the publisher, except for the inclusion of brief quotations in a review.

The "Getting Your Voice Heard" material on pages 82-86 appear courtesy of John Wiley & Sons, Inc. and first appeared as "10 Tips for Being Heard by Others" in *2007 Pfeiffer Annual - Training*. Edited by Elain Biech.

Copyright © 2009 by Multi-Media Publications Inc.

Paperback	ISBN-10: 1-895186-60-9	ISBN-13: 9781895186604
Adobe PDF ebook	ISBN-10: 1-895186-61-7	ISBN-13: 9781895186611
Palm PDB ebook	ISBN-10: 1-895186-62-5	ISBN-13: 9781895186628
Microsoft LIT ebook	ISBN-10: 1-895186-63-3	ISBN-13: 9781895186635
Mobipocket PRC ebook	ISBN-10: 1-895186-64-1	ISBN-13: 9781895186642

Published in Canada. Printed simultaneously in the United States of America and in England.

CIP data available from the publisher.

Table of Contents

Foreword 5
Introduction 7
Chapter 1
   Let's Make a Deal 11
Chapter 2
   Getting What You Really Want in Life ... 19
Chapter 3
   Taking Charge of Your Life 59
Chapter 4
   Communicating Successfully 89
Chapter 5
   Strategic Relationships 103
Chapter 6
   Finding Your Life Strategy 129
Chapter 7
   Negotiating Life Strategies 145

Foreword

As a Human Resources professional for nearly thirty years, I have been involved in the lives of many different people in a wide variety of situations. I have worked with countless employees over these years as they have gone through personal and work-related problems. Helping these employees deal with the loss of a loved one, the birth of a child, sickness and illness, financial problems, legal problems, issues in the workplace, and many other challenging situations, you learn a great deal about people. One's personal life and career often become intertwined during difficult, as well as happy, times. There are few, if any, events that occur in an employee's life that do not affect his or her employment in some manner and in which a Human Resources person would not get involved. Much of this book is based on these observations about people as I have worked with them in my professional role in a wide variety of situations.

Through these many interactions, I have had a glimpse into people's lives from an often very personal perspective. What I have observed is that people approach their lives in many different ways. Each person views life from a unique perspective. What I learned was that there was a distinction concerning people's attitudes about being successful in life. I began to see a definite difference between those with a positive attitude about being successful in life and those who had a poor attitude or outlook about life.

Winning Either Way

Although this may seem obvious or intuitive, I noticed definite patterns to these differences.

I remember an employee who had a child that was critically ill at the time. I worked closely with this employee to assist with medical coverage and time off from work to care for the child. I noticed throughout this period of the child's illness an unusually positive attitude on the part of the employee concerning the outcome of this situation. This employee had no doubt that her child would fully recover and lead a normal and healthy life despite medical evidence to the contrary. I saw the child on several occasions during this illness and noticed that the child also had a very positive outlook, as did all the other members of their family. There was never ever any doubt in my mind that the child's full recovery was due in large measure from the entire family's positive attitudes.

Experiences like this really make you wonder about the power of positive thinking. Is it truly possible to achieve the results you want in life simply by thinking positively about these occurrences? Moreover, what happens if despite all your positive thoughts, you do not get what you want? How do you continue to think positively despite failure? I began to notice that how you define success has a lot to do with how you feel about the results you achieve. People too often have a very narrow view about how they would define success and failure. The distinctions are usually very clear to them. However, the truth I believe that I have noticed is that these distinctions are not so easily defined. There really is not such a bright line between success and failure in life. It is often a matter of perspective.

I am not suggesting that people should be satisfied with just anything in life or that the feelings of failure or disappointment will never exist for people. These things are indeed part of life. But falling into the syndrome of believing that success and happiness in life are dependent on external factors outside your control can become a limiting, if not debilitating, condition for many people. Changing your attitude with a more practical life strategy in which you change your expectations about winning in life can make all the difference in the world. This is what Winning Either Way is all about.

Introduction

Wouldn't it be nice to win in just about any situation we face? Of course, this would be great but it is not a very realistic objective for anyone to expect in life. Life is full of disappointments, setbacks, and even failures. This is all part of what we should expect to some degree in life. But why do some people seem always to take home the *prizes* in life? Why do they seem to get the best jobs and appear to have the best relationships and continuously be successful in just about every endeavor they attempt in life? Are they more talented, better at beating the odds, or just luckier than everyone else? The difference may be their attitude about winning. They indeed may be more determined than others are to be a winner. They may work harder to develop greater skills and talents. Perhaps even more importantly, they may have a better strategy for winning in life. This book was written to help you focus on this last point—your strategy about winning. This strategy concerning achieving your goals in life may be the most important factor in determining the success you achieve during your lifetime.

Winning Either Way does not offer a sure bet solution to all the problems you may face in life—there really is no such thing. *Winning Either Way* presents more of a philosophy, a mindset, a way of thinking about being successful in your life. *Winning Either Way* will help you look at things from a new perspective, through a different lens concerning your expectations in life. Adapting a *Winning Either Way* life strategy helps you move away from the win/lose perspective that most people are accustomed to and find ways to get something that is of value to you in just about any situation. Just as by-products in a manufacturing process, life is full of unexpected opportunities but you have to be able to see them. If life gives you lemons, you should go into the lemonade business, sell stock, become rich, get your own plane, buy a private island, or whatever makes you happy. What you might think is the worst thing can ultimately become the best thing. Losing in its traditional sense is not always a bad thing. Change can bring unexpected opportunities. Second chances often ultimately and ironically offer better opportunities.

Winning Either Way will help you better understand what winning really is and is not. Winning as typically defined may not always get you what you really want. The problem is that we often have unrealistic or impractical views about winning. Winning is often thought of as a singularly exclusive event. Either we win or we lose. Winning is reserved for only one fortunate person or group of people. Everyone else is at a loss. This extremely limiting perception about winning is the cause of much frustration, anxiety, and stress for many. It creates that classic win/lose mentality that describes how so many people have been taught to think. I am either a winner or a loser, with the default position being loser. Losing often becomes an expected outcome in many or most of life's endeavors for many. Winning is limited to the best of the best. This viewpoint is understandable considering the fact that in most competitions in life only one winner is awarded the top distinction; that is if you become invested in this win/lose mentality throughout your life. The main point of this book is that you can change your perspective about winning. It does not have to be limited to an elite few in every contest or situation in life.

Introduction

We love to see and hear about people turning around their lives in rags to riches stories. Media news programs such as *60 Minutes* often feature these stories about everyday people becoming rich and famous by working hard in life or getting that big break that propels them into the public spotlight. We get personal accounts of often intimate and personal details of their lives that typically are only available to their families and closest friends. We see and hear about people overcoming adversities that are hard for most of us to imagine, including health issues, family or financial problems, economic disadvantages, prejudice, and a multitude of other problems. Their stories inspire us to deal more effectively with the problems we face and to appreciate the advantages we have had in our lives.

Even television commercials are full of stories of real people turning their lives around. For instance, the fast food restaurant chain Subway features people on its television commercials that have lost huge amounts of weight eating their products that are lower in fat and calories than other fast food products on the market. One of its key spokespersons, a young man named Jared, has risen to celebrity status because of these testimonials to eating Subway's sub sandwiches. Jared turned his previous weight problem into a career and life-changing event. It is doubtful that Jared ever dreamed during his heftier days of the positive impact his weight problem would eventually have on his life. But life can change for us in many unexpected ways.

The phenomenal success of the television show *American Idol* is further evidence of just how much we love to see others strive to reach their goals in life. Countless wannabe rising stars all vie for a shot at becoming the next American Idol despite, in many cases, a complete lack of any singing talent. Winners of this contest each year have gone on to great fame and stardom. But sometimes the winner is not the one who gets the most attention. Runners-up in this contest have also gained the attention of the viewing audience and have gone on to success that rivals even that of the winners.

Winning Either Way

The point is that success is not always a "winner-take-all" scenario. Coming in second place does not mean that we have failed. It depends on how we look at it. If we walk away without the top prize feeling as if we have failed, then we probably have failed. But if we consider just how difficult it was to get to this spot and how close we came to winning, we might see things in a different light. The real question we should be asking ourselves is how we can capitalize on the success we have reached, not how did we fail to win the contest or competition. This is what truly differentiates real winners from losers. Winners find a way to be successful, no matter what.

Creating a more effective life strategy may require us to redefine what *winning* really means to us. We might not always *win* in the traditional sense, but we still may be able to get something we really want or even something of greater value than originally sought. The key is to find ways to turn situations into positives or even a *win redefined* no matter what happens in our lives. Winning truly is a state of mind not an absolute, as most people think.

CHAPTER **1**

Let's Make a Deal

Life is really a series of negotiations and compromises. We are constantly bargaining for what we want in life. Unfortunately, we often settle for less than we really want during these negotiations. *Winning Either Way* is designed to help you find better ways to negotiate what you really want in life.

Think about all the things that you actually negotiate with others in your daily life. You negotiate a great deal more than you might realize. Almost everything you do is a negotiation of one kind or another. You even negotiate with yourself!

"Am I going to have that piece of pie or not?" is a typical *self-negotiation,* as you make a private deal with yourself that you will go to the gym the next day to burn off those extra calories. Keeping this deal with yourself may be another story depending on your determination to keep off those extra pounds.

These daily negotiations go beyond ourselves and spill over to many of our daily activities. We are constantly negotiating just about everything we do in our lives. For example, the following is a typical negotiation between a child and a parent that undoubtedly plays out every night in millions of homes:

Winning Either Way

"Honey, it's time for you to go to bed."

"Mommy, can't I stay up just a little bit longer?"

"No, it's time to go to bed now."

"Please, can't I watch the rest of the TV show? Please, please, please! I promise that I will go to bed as soon as it is over."

"All right, but you need to promise that you will go right to bed as soon as it is over."

"I promise, Mommy!"

There is no denying that this was a negotiation about the child's bedtime that evening. The mother submitted her proposal and the child presented a counterproposal. They came to an agreement based on the new terms presented by each party. We may not normally think of the natural give-and-take that occurs constantly in our lives as negotiations, but it really is just that.

We are already much more skilled at negotiating what we really want in life than we may realize. Much of our daily routines in life are negotiation-based in some form. Where we shop to find the best price is a negotiation of sorts. We bargain with our purchasing dollars every day. Commercials and advertisements are really a negotiation with the consumer. These messages present us with the opportunity to enjoy the benefits of the product or service if we in return make the purchase. Either we accept their proposal to purchase the product or service or we reject the proposal. The collective consumer-purchasing dollar is the ultimate negotiation bargaining chip for billions and billions of dollars each day.

Life's negotiations come in all sizes and shapes. A major negotiation that we typically encounter in life is buying a new car. What a negotiation game this really is. Unlike almost other big-ticket items that we purchase with fixed price tags attached such as washers, dryers, television sets, etc., purchasing a car is often a confusing and even intimidating event for many people. Doing our homework and understanding exactly what the profit margin is for the dealer, is critically important to getting the best deal we possibly can. We also need to understand the lingo involved in this transaction. What exactly does "dealer invoice" really mean? What extras should we be willing to pay for in addition to the deal we make, or what should we insist is included in the price we finally agree upon? We need to know to ask about such add-ons as dealer prep or other service charges that might be slipped in just before we sign on the dotted line and drive our new car away for slightly more money than we thought we were going to pay.

Another negotiation that most people face at some time in their lives is purchasing a new home. This is usually the biggest investment that a person will ever make in their entire lifetime. Myriad details and factors need to be considered when negotiating this magnitude of a deal. Location, taxes, condition of the home, repairs that may be needed, terms of the loan, insurance costs, schools, contingencies, and many other factors all must be considered when discussing price with a seller or real estate agent.

The problem that most people face when entering into these types of major negotiations in life is that they do it so infrequently. We might purchase a car every five to seven years or even less often. We might only buy one or possibly two homes in our entire lifetime. Most of us do not really have a negotiations mentality when it comes to making most of the decisions, both big and small, during our lives. We typically consider the options presented to us and agree to that which appears to be the best option. However, often other options may not have been presented to us that might be better deals for us. Most of the time, these options are simple or even obvious if we give them some thought. We can get many things in life simply by asking, but we have to ask.

Becoming a better negotiator can help us feel more in control of our lives. Getting better deals is one way to feel like we are winning in life. It just does not make sense not to get the best that we can whenever possible. However, our attitude towards these negotiations is also important. Going into any negotiation with a win/lose mentality may be like putting everything on the line in a winner take all contest.

We also constantly face micro-issues that we negotiate every day of our lives. These involve small but still important issues and decisions. For example, you may casually discuss with a colleague or friend when you will get together.

"Let's get together later today."

"Sounds good, should we meet at 2 or at 3?"

"Doesn't really matter to me; I am available all afternoon."

"Ok, if it is all the same to you, let's make it 3. I have an earlier appointment and don't want to be rushed."

"Fine, I'll see you at 3."

In this conversation, one person conceded the decision concerning when to meet to the other. This is perfectly all right as long as that individual really did not care if their meeting was to be at 2:00 or 3:00. Is it possible that this person really did not have a preference concerning what time this meeting was to occur? Maybe, but it is also likely that this person did have a preference but did not express it when given the opportunity.

The problem is that often people agree to do things that are not perfectly all right with them. Perhaps pressure to conform or be agreeable causes us often to concede to that which we do not really want. Alternatively, we convince ourselves that we do not really care about something when we really do. What if the person who suggested this meeting really wanted to meet earlier rather than later that afternoon? How should he or she have handled this conversation? Would it have really been that much different if the dialog went like this?

"Let's get together later today."

"Sounds good, should we meet at 2 or at 3?"

"I am available all afternoon but if it's all the same to you, I would prefer to meet earlier."

"Ok, I have an earlier appointment but I will be done with that by 2."

"Fine, I'll see you at 2."

Think about these two negotiations. Each resulted in a different outcome concerning the time for the meeting, and in all likelihood, each was just as acceptable to either party. The question of whether the meeting was to be set at 2 or 3 really may not have been a big deal to anyone in this example but it does illustrate how we can go from a passive position to a more assertive position without a great deal of effort or force. In this case, both parties "won" in the sense that they were able to schedule the meeting that they both apparently wanted to be scheduled. The point is that many people often capitulate on these seemingly minor negotiations in life when they really do have a preference that they are not stating. This can lead to a feeling of constantly "losing" in life's negotiations that is not necessary or warranted.

Think about the countless other *micro-negotiations* that you encounter every day. Things such as who is going to drive, what to order for lunch, even work assignments are all often presented to us in some form of negotiation in which we have some control of the outcome. In many or most of these situations, you may not have a huge stake in the outcome or final decision. You may consider that you will *win either way* because you do not really have a preference. If this is the case, then you are well on your way to really understanding the concepts presented in this book. However, if you feel that you are constantly compromising what you really want or always seem to have to settle for your second choice, you need to rethink your life negotiations strategy. Each of these micro- negotiations culminates into bigger issues collectively, particularly if a pattern exists that involves conceding small but still important issues and decisions in your life.

This may also carry over into not so micro issues in your life as well. It may involve how much time off you get at work or when this time is granted. It could involve very important issues such as getting the job offer or promotion you have worked so hard to earn. It may also affect the quality of your relationships with others in your life. In any case, the principles and concepts presented in this book can help you negotiate what you really want better, be they big or small issues in life.

Getting what you really want in life is often a matter of strategy and thinking ahead. You need to prepare for life's negotiations ahead of time. If you do not think about it until the moment you have to decide, it will be too late. You will have to settle simply for what you get or feel that you are constantly getting the default. This may be ok if you are content with this. If not, read on. Your attitude about what you get from life is important to the results you achieve.

Learning to Say "No"

Jerry Clements had learned to be a good negotiator in some aspects of his life. He spent hours on the internet researching just about every purchase he made for his family and him. His family often got frustrated because Jerry's research sometimes caused considerable delays in these purchases as he read up on all the comparison products to choose from, weighed arguments for buying each one, and studied their Consumer Report Ratings. When he recently purchased a new family car, he knew exactly all of the dealer's costs and markups and armed with this information, negotiated a great deal on an SUV.

However, Jerry was not so diligent when it came to negotiating relationships. He constantly felt that other people were taking advantage of him. His wife described Jerry as a "giver," meaning that he always seemed to give into other people's wishes. At work, he was constantly being stuck with the duties that nobody else wanted to do in the office, most of which he got little or no credit for. He was the one who always had to organize the company outings or collect money from coworkers for a donation that the office was making or many other chores that everyone else refused to do. Even at home, he could not say "no" to his children's requests, something that caused his wife great frustration as she often had to be the one to finally put her foot down.

Jerry had always been this way; it just seemed to be part of his nature. He just never seemed to learn to be more aggressive in his relationships with others in his life. He seemed to put all these tendencies into purchases, not relationships. Obviously, he had learned to be a good negotiator in this one aspect of his life but had never learned to transfer these skills to his relationships. This did cause considerable problems for him, as he was often frustrated with himself for not refusing to do these things.

Jerry finally decided that he needed to do something about this problem. He sought help to learn to become more assertive about expressing himself and saying "no" when he really wanted to refuse to do something. Jerry learned that saying "no" was an acceptable answer if it was how he really felt. He learned to use his considerable negotiations skills to reach interpersonal agreements that were more acceptable to everyone involved—especially him.

Life Strategy Questions

- Think about some of the things in your life that you could negotiate better for yourself. What would be the result of improving these negotiations? How much of an impact could this make on your life?

- The following are suggestions for you to consider about the things that you negotiate in your life. Add to this list as appropriate for you.

- If you have financial investments, are you really getting the highest rate of return that you possibly can? From whom can you get advice that could help you get a better return on your investments?

- If you own a home, can you negotiate a better interest rate on your loan? Can you refinance? Is there a better type of loan that you should be considering?

- If you are employed, are there things that you could ask for at work that would help you perform your job better? Are you in a position to ask for a raise or better benefits? Are there better opportunities that you can bid on or ask for in your organization? Are there better opportunities outside of work that you could be considering?

- If you are about to make a major purchase or even a minor one, is there a better price that you could get somewhere else or from where you are about to make this purchase?

- Are there aspects of your relationships with others that you would like to negotiate? How could proposing these things improve your relationship(s)?

CHAPTER 2

Getting What You Really Want in Life

Getting what you really want in life is often a matter of exercising the options that are available to you. You have more opportunities and choices than you may typically think but you have to make good choices. However, many people have problems even seeing that these opportunities exist, much less taking advantage of them. They are stuck in a rut or pattern of not getting what they want out of life.

The problem is that many people fall into something that is called the *victim mentality syndrome*. Victim mentality means that someone feels as if he or she has been, or currently is, a victim of the actions of other people. These *other people* may be immediate family members, friends, colleagues, bosses, parents, or other authority figures. Victims feel that they have little or no control over their lives, that the decisions of others cause all of their problems, and that they cannot change this situation. They simply accept what happens to them as their fate in life determined by the actions and decisions of others.

However, this victim-mentality-syndrome pattern can be broken. You can take back control of your life. You do not have to be at the mercy of the decisions and actions of others. You can learn to make good decisions that are in your best interest. You do not have to let others make all your decisions for you. You can get what you want to get out of life or at least come closer to your goals than you may presently think you can. It is really a matter of your attitude concerning what you will and will not accept in life. You can have a more satisfying life but you may need to change the way you approach the challenges you face. The following model will help you begin to make this transition from victim to being more in control of what happens in your life.

Life Strategies Hierarchy

The Life Strategies Hierarchy shown below shows six different approaches to dealing with the problems or challenges we face in life. Each of the steps in the hierarchy is progressive. In other words, each step represents greater independence or personal control over the situation.

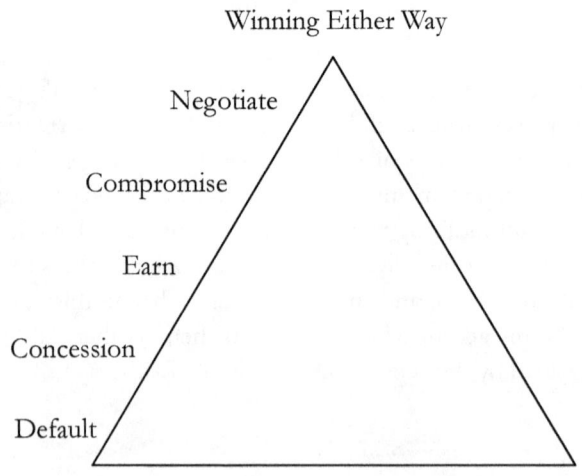

Default

Let's begin at the bottom of the hierarchy. Defaults are what you get in life if you do not make decisions yourself. A default is typically what someone else decides or determines what you will get in life. They are like consolation prizes presented to contestants who do not win the big prize in one of those television game shows. Constantly accepting life's defaults is adapting a defeatist attitude. This is paramount to saying that that you are willing to accept whatever comes your way without challenge. This is more than just being agreeable; it is being overly passive in your expectations and goals in life. It is abdication of what is important to you in life. The question you should be asking yourself is if life's defaults are ok with you. Are you satisfied just taking what comes and not doing anything substantially to change the outcome? Granted, there may be times and a circumstance in life when accepting a default is the best and most practical approach. Some things are just not worth worrying about or are not controllable, but a problem exists when this becomes a pattern in one's life. It becomes a learned helplessness and you lose control of your life.

As you read the following story about Angela, think about how she might have managed her life differently rather than constantly accepting defaults instead of what she may have really wanted.

Angela's Story

Angela felt like she was caught in a rut. She was constantly compromising her wants and desires in life. It was not that Angela was afraid to speak up or step forward; it was that she always seemed to be too late. By the time Angela got around to making her wishes known, what she sought seemed to be already gone. She constantly was in second, third, or fourth place when it came to getting the rewards in life.

Winning Either Way

> When she was in school, she constantly was being told that the special assignment or activity she hoped to participant in had been given to someone else. All that seemed ever to be left for her to do was what nobody else wanted. For example, she would have to settle for the science fair project that was the least interesting or least likely to garner an award. Or, she would end up going to the big school dance with the guy that everyone else turned down for a date.
>
> After graduation, Angela applied for many good jobs but she was constantly told that someone else better qualified had been selected. This was despite Angela's good academic record in a difficult field of study that should have qualified her for the jobs she sought after graduation. She finally landed a mediocre job and began looking for a house to purchase. Angela again never seemed to be able to get that house that she really wanted—always being outbid by someone else or too late in making an offer.
>
> And so it went for Angela. She never really seemed to get what she wanted or deserved in life. She did not have such a terrible life; she just always seemed disappointed or ripped off in some way or another. Angela often wondered how she could change her life and get what she really wanted. She felt like she was caught in a vicious cycle of always getting the minimum of what she deserved rather than really reaching out for what she really wanted out of life.

What do you think about this story about Angela's life? Do you think that Angela was just a victim of the circumstances that constantly surrounded her? After all, there is a lot of competition for the rewards in life. You cannot always come out on top, and often you need to settle for what is available. Is that really such a bad thing? Before you answer this question, consider an important point. Angela was not unhappy with her plight in life. However, she felt, perhaps rightfully so, that she deserved better. She obviously felt that others were getting what she worked for and deserved in life. Why was there this constant pattern of not getting what she really wanted? How could Angela have managed her life differently to achieve and receive what she really wanted?

The answer to these questions may be found in the next steps in the model. As you examine these steps, think back to this story about Angela and ask yourself how she could have applied these concepts in her life to achieve different results possibly.

Concession

The next step in the hierarchy is concession. Concession is a common life strategy mentality that is a part of the way most people learn to look at life. Concession means that you have given up to some degree on reaching a goal or objective. We live in a competitive world with limited rewards available. People are constantly vying for these coveted life prizes. Becoming frustrated with not getting the rewards you seek in life creates a concession mentality for many.

The way that things are structured in much of life supports this limited rewards perspective. Sports provide many examples of limited rewards. Sporting events are designed for someone to win and someone to lose. That is what creates competition. It is what makes sporting events exciting and challenging. How much fun would it be if there were not some kind of competition among teams or players to be victorious? The obvious answer is that it would not be very much fun to watch or play in a sporting event where there was no competition. However, it is also not much fun to watch a team stop really trying to win and concede victory to the other side. Even the most ardent of football fans begin to leave the stadium when one team is running away with victory and the competition is over before the end of the game.

However, having a concession mentality is not necessarily a bad thing. It fits well into much of the way that society functions. It is an easily understandable approach to life. Someone is always going to win at the expense of others. You cannot fall apart every time you do not get what you want in life. You must be able to accept not reaching your goals and be able to continue to move forward still with a positive attitude. Winning is fun and usually results in rewards, but what if you do not always win? What would happen if you found yourself repeatedly on the losing end? How might you feel about having a concession mentality under these circumstances?

However, constant concession is not effective life strategy—at least not long-term. This is the inherent problem with this mindset that so many people adapt. They have an "all or nothing" attitude. In this case, you are really putting all of your chips on winning, but life is not typically structured this way. As mentioned, there are limited winners for most of the sought after and desirable things in life. Adapting a life strategy based solely on a win mentality is paramount to setting yourself up for disappointment and a constant state of concession.

Learned Concession

Frank Johnson had adapted a concession attitude at work because of many years of being disappointed in his career. He had been passed over for countless promotions that he felt he deserved. He was not sure how he got into this career rut; it just seemed to sneak up on him. He had started his career with what seemed to be great promise. Early on, he seemed to get the attention of the right people in the company and had every reason to believe that he might be on the fast track for promotions in the future. The turning point seemed to be a job that had become available that he really wanted during his first few months with the company. The buzz around the office was that Frank was a sure bet to get the job. Every time he saw his boss, he anticipated being offered

> this great opportunity. But this discussion never transpired. It was announced that someone else was getting the job. Rumors were that this person had some kind of connection to the CEO or something like that. Frank was devastated. He just never seemed to regain his confidence and this soon became apparent to others, including his boss and other decision makers in the organization. He was constantly being passed over for promotion after promotion until he got to the point where he no longer had any expectation of advancing in the company.

You could end up with a defeatist attitude because of constantly being disappointed by not winning the prizes you seek in life. Just as Frank in the previous story, in time, you might stop trying as hard if you begin to expect a less than winning result for your efforts. This can make it tough if you tend to look at things in life this way. But there are other ways of looking at life. You do not have to depend constantly on coming out on top in winner-take-all competitions to feel worthy and good about yourself. You can adapt other strategies to give you more control over your life.

Earn

Earn is the next step up in on the hierarchy. As its name implies, this step involves earning what you get in life. Certain things cannot be given to you, but rather you have to earn them. The process of trying to circumvent this step, although one too frequently attempted, is not usually a very successful strategy. Earning is different from competing in some ways but not in all ways. To clarify, you do need to earn the ability to be competitive. You earn this by working hard to gain the skills and expertise necessary to be successful. The difference in this step in the process is that it does not focus so much on a single event or series of events that define winners and losers.

Winning Either Way

Earn as presented as this step in the process is more about doing those things in life that result in achieving the goals and rewards you deserve in life. Earn in this sense involves less risk than the subsequent steps. Earn describes what you get in life from dedication, perseverance, and hard work. Earn is not necessarily a sure bet. People do work hard to earn what they want in life but still do not achieve their goals. However, that does not mean that you have to concede your goals or accept default. When you work hard to earn something, you do not normally give up your goals so easily or quickly. However, the chances of reaching your life's goals are much greater if you adapt this life philosophy. If, for example, instead of working towards earning life's rewards, you instead count on winning the lottery, you are headed for almost certain disappointment. Yes, people do win the lottery, but the chances of this happening to you are certainly not in your favor. If you really want to increase your chances of being successful in life, you most likely will have to earn it.

Henry's Hard Work Pays Off

Henry Goodson learned from an early age that he had to earn his way in this world. He came from a working class family where both his parents toiled hard just to make ends meet for their three sons of which Henry was the oldest. His father worked as a mechanic in an electronics factory where he started at the age of eighteen and his mother worked as a cashier at the local supermarket. From the time he was twelve years old, Henry began delivering papers, cutting grass for neighbors, and performing any other odd jobs he could get around the neighborhood to earn extra money.

As soon as he was old enough, he got his first real paying job at a fast food restaurant. He saved his money to pay for part of his college education and took out student loans for the remaining portions. In college, he worked hard to earn his degree

> in engineering, graduating at the top of his class. He went directly from college to the job market, finding an excellent opportunity with a top corporation where he started as a project engineer. Through the company's educational assistance program, he earned his MBA and quickly rose through the managerial ranks to an executive level by the time he was forty years old. Henry never felt that he should have done anything but work hard in his life. He believed that hard work, which he did, is the key to living a full and rewarding life.
>
> Even though he was able to provide his family more financially than his parents had been able to provide him and his brothers, Henry did not believe in pampering his children. He required his children to work for any extra money they wanted as they grew up and to pay for a portion of their college education even though he could afford to pay their tuition bills. Henry believed that they would value and appreciate the opportunity to go to college more if they paid for part of the bill.

As you review the remaining steps of this hierarchy, note that the next three all involve strategies that assume that an individual has earned his or her ability to move to these levels. Earning your way in life from this point on the model is an assumption. In other words, you need to have already adapted the philosophy that you need to earn what you get in life in order to reach these next steps.

Compromise

Compromise is when you agree to certain concessions or gains that you negotiate in some manner. However, in life's compromises, you are not always keenly aware that you are compromising. Going back to the earlier example of negotiating a meeting time, these decisions often are based on a compromise of the two proposals presented.

"I'm available at 2 today; can we meet then?"

"I'm sorry, but I'm busy at 2 with another commitment. Can we meet later in the afternoon?"

"No, I'm busy the rest of the afternoon. How about we meet in the morning?"

"Ok, I guess I can rearrange some things. Let's plan on meeting at 11."

"I will see you at 11."

In this brief dialog, neither person gets his or her first choice for a meeting time. Both had to compromise in order to find an acceptable meeting time for both of them. We are constantly compromising, consciously or unconsciously, these kinds of things each day. We do not always get our first choice. For example, you may not get the seat you wanted on the morning commuter bus or train, the coffee shop may not have your favorite muffin, you may not get seats you wanted for the big game this weekend, or the car that you had finally decided to purchase may no longer be available and you have to settle for another model. Life is indeed full of compromises.

Most of these compromises involve those *micro-issues* such as those described above. None of these issues will substantially change your life. You may have to settle for a piece of fruit or yogurt, a much healthier breakfast than that muffin or find that you really like the car that you settled for instead of your first choice. In these instances, you might come to realize that sometimes not getting your first choice turns out to be better in the end. The reality is that many different acceptable choices to many of the decisions that we make in our lives probably exist on a daily basis. We would be just as satisfied with any of the options available. We often do not really know precisely what we want. We make choices often capriciously without giving any real thought to the matter.

However, there are times when we are faced with the prospect of compromising on things that are important to us. Most people just will not compromise some things, no matter what. These may involve principles or standards for ourselves that are not optional. For most people, their morals and beliefs are not subject to compromise. We will not do certain things that would be inconsistent with our convictions, regardless of the circumstances. However, other situations we face in life pose less of a moral dilemma to us and are subject to compromise.

One example is the work/life balance that many working people face today. Most people do not begin their careers intending to spend exorbitant amounts of time working at the expense of spending less time with their families. However, the pressures to succeed, spurred by financial needs and myriad other factors, often drive upwardly mobile professionals to compromise family time for career advancement. They spend long hours at the office or traveling on business in order to advance their careers. This is actually a significant compromise that many working spouses and parents make today. This is a complicated compromise the individual rationalizes by as being for the good of the family financially—an important consideration today. This is fine as long as everyone is comfortable with the compromise—but sometimes this is not the case.

Work Takes Over

Julie and Sam Whitaker wanted to make a good life for their family. From the time they were married, they dreamed of buying a nice home, cars, vacations, and all the things that make life a little more enjoyable. They lived in an expensive part of the country, making obtaining all of these things more of a challenge. In fact, both Julie and Sam needed to work outside the home in order to be able to afford these things. As they raised their family, they both continued to work as many couples do today. Finding time to be together as a family was always a challenge with their

> *busy lives. The responsibilities of work combined with the kids' school and other activities pretty much took all of their time. They seldom had any time to spend together as a family. They were always rushing off for a business appointment or to soccer practice, a dance recital, or something. Julie and Sam worried that they did not spend enough time just being together as a family. They did not feel that they had the same relationship with their children as they had had with their parents, taking family vacations together each year and having dinner as a family each evening. Something seemed to be missing in their lives with their hectic schedules.*

Compromise is not a bad thing as long as you are comfortable with what you are compromising. Compromise allows things to happen that probably would not have been possible otherwise. However, compromise is not a good life strategy if you feel denied or cheated in some way in the deal as the Whitakers in the previous story did. Only you can decide if you are satisfied with the compromises you make in life.

Negotiate

Negotiate is the next step in the hierarchy. As discussed earlier, we negotiate many micro-issues in our lives often without being conscious that we are negotiating. We all gain a certain expertise and comfortableness in these negotiations. However, what is meant by "negotiate" in this model can be something quite different. We are not talking here about negotiating a time to meet a friend or colleague but actually negotiating big events in your life. These are major negotiations. Even when making critical life decisions, we do not always examine all of our options or the potential consequences of these decisions. We sometimes accept or even default to what others expect us to do. We may not exercise options that may be readily available. We sometimes are reluctant to ask or question the system. We are gently coerced into agreeing for the sake of appearing agreeable. We do not want to *rock the boat*, so to speak.

We are often faced with many negotiations in our lives that we may not always be really prepared to address. A commonly negotiated agreement that we are presented is to *split the difference*. In other words, if there is a difference, for example, in price, we agree to meet halfway. Say you want to purchase something that might be negotiable, such as a car. The seller wants $20,000; you offer $18,000. In an attempt to settle this difference, the seller proposes that you split the difference between the asking price and the offering price and you agree to a price of $19,000. Seems fair enough, right? Well, maybe, but look at it this way—you already had a counteroffer by the seller for $19,000. What would have happened if you had continued to negotiate for an even better price? Would the seller have agreed to $18,500? There is only one way to find out—ask.

Negotiators that do this for a living typically have a plan, a result that they strive to reach, an end in mind. They know what they want and what they are willing to settle for or walk away. They know what they have to put at risk as well as the potential rewards for what they put at stake. Everything in negotiations is a two-way street. If you want something, then you have to give something in return. They negotiate about issues that others may have conceded or given away without asking for anything in return. They do not give anything away free. Good negotiators enter negotiations confident of their ability to get the results they desire. They know the facts. They also know the parameters of the negotiations. They have already predetermined what they are willing to settle for and what they are not. The negotiations themselves are in many ways merely a formality, as the negotiator has already decided what he or she will agree and not agree to during these proceedings. Negotiators come prepared to deal with any number of different scenarios that they must face. They look their competition in the eye and state what it is they expect to receive at the end of the negotiations.

Winning Either Way

What would happen if you were a more effective negotiator for what you seek in life? Do you think that you would or could reach more of your goals in life? What would happen if you approached life more from a negotiations mindset? How might things be different for you? For example, what if instead of just settling for what life brings your way, you set clear defined goals for what you want to achieve during your lifetime? And what do you think might happen if you constantly worked towards negotiating in some way to reach these goals on a regular or even daily basis? Do you think that you would be more or less likely to reach these goals? Is it not likely that this strategy would be significantly more likely to yield the desired results you seek in life?

What would these life negotiations actually look like? To begin with, the first thing that a negotiation involves is a request or even a demand for something. As they say—if you do not ask, you will never receive. A big part of changing your mindset about what you can negotiate for yourself in life is getting over the fear of asking for what you want in life. We are often afraid to ask because we do not want to be told we cannot have something or be turned down. Alternatively, we might be embarrassed to ask because of the fear that we will not be taken seriously or even be ridiculed for even thinking that we could achieve our goals. However, every negotiation begins with a want, a desire, or even a dream. You need to first conceptualize your goals and then strive to reach for them. You cannot be reluctant or even afraid to let others know what you hope to achieve in life. This is the first step towards negotiating your life. The next step is to find out what you need to do to begin reaching these goals.

These negotiations could be with others who control or influence the results you achieve in life. These negotiations might even be with you. You could set varying goals for yourself that you want to reach in your life and adjust these goals as necessary depending on the progress you are making towards achieving these objectives. These goals could be negotiated both up and down depending on the negotiating strength you might find within yourself. Negotiating strength is determined by the leverage you might have at any given time in the negotiation process to gain what you seek in negotiations. For example, if you own a home that you wish to sell that is in great demand by potential buyers, you would be in a strong negotiations position. However, if you own a home in a real estate market where there are few, if any, potential buyers, you would be in a weak negotiations position. Putting this in the context of negotiating what you personally want in life, if you have any number of options available to you concerning a life decision, you would be in a stronger negotiations position. Similarly, if you have few viable options, you would be in a weaker negotiating position.

However, even when you find yourself in a weaker negotiating position, certain negotiable things still exist. Identifying and exercising these negotiation options are the keys to truly negotiating your life. For example, think about what might be negotiable when receiving a job offer. Starting pay might be something that could be discussed, even negotiated, with the prospective employer.

"Yes, I am very interested in the position but I was hoping to start at a higher salary. In fact, I do have another opportunity available to me that pays 10 percent more than what you have offered me for this position. If you could increase the starting salary by this amount, I would take the job."

What do you think that the likelihood of this prospective employer raising the starting salary might be? Of course, this would depend on any number of factors, including the organization's salary policies, but you would think that there is a chance that this job candidate might get a higher starting salary based on this negotiation. One word of caution about this or any negotiations—do not bluff. In other words, do not take an all-or-nothing position unless you are prepared to walk

Winning Either Way

away from the deal. If this job candidate really needed this job to support his or her family, putting the offer on the line for more money probably would not be a good negotiating strategy. Neither would it be to fabricate the other offer or opportunity to a prospective employer. You might just hear the following:

"Well, we're sorry but our policy is not to negotiate starting salaries with candidates for employment with our company. Good luck with this other job opportunity and in your future career."

Negotiation on this hierarchy is intended to be utilized in those situations where you are in a position to negotiate. It is when you have other options or you would not be risking something that you cannot afford to lose. Negotiations should be reserved for those situations in which you have leverage without risking something that you do not want to lose. Going back to the job offer example, this approach should only be used if you truly do have another opportunity that you are interested in that does pay more money, if you are going to make accepting the offer contingent on the salary increase. However, this job candidate could have asked for the increase in starting salary in a less demanding way indicating that it was not an all-or-nothing proposition, but this would have weakened his or her negotiating position. The job candidate might also negotiate other things. Things such as starting date, vacation time, office location, benefits, etc. all could be negotiated perhaps more easily than salary. It just takes a negotiation orientation to getting more of what you want in life.

Think of the countless situations in life in which you could ask for something more and likely get what you want just for the asking. Think about services that might be available that you purchase on a daily basis, which are willing to provide something more if requested at no extra charge most of the time. For example, retailers often provide many services free of charge just for the asking by a customer. Deliveries, discounts, return services, guarantees, etc—these are all forms of negotiations available just for the asking.

Keep in mind that the word "negotiate" also means to navigate. In this sense, you need to navigate the obstacles between you and your goals in life. There are typically many potential barriers between you and your goals. How well you negotiate these obstacles will determine largely your success and happiness in life. Negotiating these obstacles is often based on the same principles as negotiations in the give-and-take definition of this concept. Often negotiating these obstacles is a matter of taking them on. By aggressively dealing with your problems, you might just be able to solve them. You might just be able to negotiate away many of the problems you face in life, just for the asking.

Winning Either Way (WEW)

Winning Either Way is as much of a mindset as it is a strategy. Thinking from a WEW point of view leads one to see that failure is more a state of mind than a reality. You fail only if you allow others to make you believe you have failed or you begin to believe it yourself. WEW helps you see that there are many ways to win not just the traditional winner-take-all scenarios. WEW helps you understand that not winning is different from losing and that all it really means is that your goal, or goals, has simply not yet been met. An experience in which you have not met an objective should be thought of as more of a learning experience than a failure. Finishing in a position other than first is not the worst thing that can happen. So much work and effort goes into competing that never get credit unless you come out "number one." This is not only not giving credit where credit is due but also ignoring everything that everyone but the declared winner has accomplished. If you are stuck in this mindset, then you are not giving yourself the credit that you really deserve. Contrary to what many believe, winning is not everything or the only thing.

Winning Either Way

Being "number two" is not the worst position to be in and might even be a more desirable position in life.

For example, using a sports analogy again, let's use the example of a professional tennis player who, during a point in his or her career, is winning just about every tournament entered. All the rewards of being the number one tennis player in the world are bestowed upon this champion. He or she receives all of the top prize money, product endorsements, fame, and other privileges and benefits that are typically part of being at the top of the game.

Others, particularly those in second, third, or fourth place finish after each tournament that he or she wins, envy this player. For these are the players who rightfully believe that they are just a few points away from receiving these top honors that this champion continuously seems to walk away with in hand.

It is not that these others' lives are being ruined by not winning these tournaments or that they have lives that different from that of the champion. They earn good money on the tour, experience a good deal of notoriety, do what they really enjoy for a living, and are constantly striving to improve their game. They may also think about other things other than tennis. Realistically, they may need to consider other ways to earn a living than playing tennis. They may have more time to spend with friends and family than the champion who is constantly being barraged by the press and fans for interviews, autographs, and pictures.

In many ways, their quality of life may actually be better than the champion's. They do not feel the pressure each time they step onto the tennis court to perform at an outstanding level. They have less to prove or defend. During tournaments, they may be better able to enjoy the competitive experience and camaraderie of the other players. And they still have something to strive for—becoming the number one player even though if they ever do reach this goal, they may find it not to be everything it is cracked up to be.

This is not to say that aspiring to be the number one tennis player in the world is not a good thing. As mentioned, to the contrary, it obviously has many wonderful benefits. The point is that not reaching this or any other goal that you may aspire to reach is not failure or anything even remotely close. Too many efforts to reach the top spot or position are dismissed as something less than unsuccessful if not victorious. Too many excellent efforts by those other than the winner often do not get the credit they deserve. WEW is about recognizing everything good that you do even when not completely successful in your efforts. WEW is about giving yourself credit for everything good that you do regardless of the outcome or results. This is what helps you perform better the next time.

Often the competitor who continuously comes in second place has the longest and most satisfying career. Staying on top may come with a price that is more costly in the end. Champions sometimes become challenged by their own accomplishments. Being in a second tier role is just not compatible with either their self-images or public personae. Not winning simply is not something acceptable. They now no longer have the luxury of being able to lose the championship gracefully, as they were formerly expected to do. Instead of being viewed as a challenger who just was not able to be victorious, they may be more perceived to be the loser. Their past victories become more haunting or a curse of sorts. Their only viable option is to retire from competition and allow their accomplishments to become a matter of record. This is fine as long as the individual is comfortable with his or her new role as a former athlete or champion and the notoriety that accompanies this status. However, their athletic accomplishments may take on a very different perspective at a later date or time, depending on how successful they make the transition from current star to former athlete.

Winning Either Way

The world of sports also provides many other excellent examples of the fickleness, as well as the resilience, of legendary status. Certain iconic sports figures seem to endure regardless of the truth that may be revealed about them. One example is the legendary baseball great, Mickey Mantle. Mickey Mantle is considered by many as one of the greatest New York Yankees of all time. He had both the talent and the persona to attract legions of fans throughout his baseball career and even for years afterwards. Nevertheless, even by Mickey's own admission and actions, he was not quite the exemplary example that he should have been, particularly for kids growing up and wanting to emulate him. His antics off the field are well known and his excessive drinking over the years, even during his baseball career, probably led to his death in 1995 at the age of 63. But all this has little affected Mickey's legendary status. Millions of baseball fans around the world still greatly revere and even worship him.

Now, consider another baseball legend—the Cincinnati Reds' Pete Rose. Rose has been ostracized from baseball for admittedly betting on the game and denied Hall of Fame status that would have certainly been bestowed upon him otherwise. It is as if Rose's gambling habit has superseded his accomplishments in baseball. His legendary status has been unceremoniously stripped from him or at least tarnished beyond repair. Other baseball players have also had their legendary status diminished because of public perceptions. Take, for example, Barry Bonds as he passed Babe Ruth's (whose legendary status is also untouchable despite his behavior off the field) career homerun record with very mixed reception from the media and fans because of his alleged performance-enhancing drug usage during the later part of his career.

Former Heisman Trophy winner and professional football great O. J. Simpson will forever be remembered for his suspected but criminally acquitted murder of his former wife Nicole Brown and her friend, rather than his athletic accomplishments. Even though Simpson was found innocent of the criminal charges of murder in court, he is still believed guilty in the eyes of the public and stripped of the adoration and, consequently, the privileges typically afforded a legendary football hero. His public image was further tarnished in 2007 when he became involved in an armed robbery in Las Vegas as he was apparently trying to retrieve sports memorabilia he believed originally stolen from him.

A WEW philosophy is about defining winning for you instead of having it defined for you, as has happened for many of the former sports stars mentioned above. Winning, to be truly satisfying, must be achieved according to your own values, standards, rules, and principles. Winning according to these criteria may be different for each person. Personal victories are typically the most rewarding in life. WEW is not abdication of your goals or lowering your standards. WEW involves setting higher standards but not feeling as if you failed if you do not reach them. You learn to be happy with what you have accomplished, and not focus so much on what you may have not. WEW is like taking a step back and looking at the big picture. WEW allows you to shed yourself of most, or at least many, of your frustrations, resentments, etc. that often accompany not getting everything what you want in life. WEW allows you to find ways to move positively forward in just about any situation. WEW helps you move forward in life rather than bogging you down with setbacks and disappointments.

The point is that we need to realize that daily problems or issues are temporary, even fleeting. Daily problems usually are not such a big deal the next day. They are replaced with the next day's problem. Looking back, they do not seem like problems after all. WEW helps you keep things in perspective and focus on that which really matters. Just imagine what this type of thinking could do for your relationships with others in your life. Instead of being bogged down in petty disagreements that often occur, you focus on your relationships and on making them stronger.

You need to keep things in their proper perspective. Sometimes we need to look at life as if we were experiencing it through other's eyes. Think about how your life might look from someone else's perspective. Others may seek the things that you take for granted. Most people spend their lives looking for something that they might not currently have and envy that which someone else has. People in modest houses look at those in expensive houses and say, "WOW, I would love to have a house like that." People in expensive houses look at those in mansions and say, "WOW, I would love to have a house like that." People in mansions look at the super wealthy and at their estates and say, "WOW, I would love to have a house like that." WEW helps us to move away from this syndrome and focus on more productive and positive things in our lives.

Kevin Smithton always seemed to want something more than what he got. Even from the time that he was a young boy, he was always striving for something better. Everyone said Kevin's competitive spirit allowed him to excel in so many different things. He was a top student in school and a star athlete playing key roles on both his high school's basketball and football teams. He went on to college where he continued his athletic career as captain of the football team and where he was considered a big man on campus. He went on to a very successful business career, becoming a top executive of a growing company before he was forty years old. To others, Kevin's life seemed like a fairy tale. He always seemed to come out on top, no matter what his endeavors. Everything seemed to come so easy for him. He seemed to have all the rewards in life.

However, from Kevin's perspective, it was not quite so ideal. Over the years, he had become a perfectionist. Perhaps this is what drove him to reach such significant accomplishments in his life. He did not let many others get a glimpse into his compulsion for perfection. To his admiring friends and colleagues, he just seemed

> to be the whiz kid who was successful in everything he did. To those who were close to him, he was an obsessed man. Kevin never really enjoyed all the rewards of the accomplishments that his many talents allowed him to achieve. Everything was always just short of meeting his expectations.
>
> Kevin continued living his life this way until one day he had a rude awaking. His wife whom he adored finally could no longer stand his demands for perfection from everyone, including his family. She threatened to leave him if he did not change. He suddenly realized that he was missing what was important in life. He began to ask himself, "What good was everything I accomplished if I am always dissatisfied? And if it cost him his family, was it worth the price?
>
> Kevin began to look at things differently. He no longer had such a narrow perspective on success. He learned that being successful could be measured in many different ways. Perfection is not necessarily success. It may actually be something less than success, for it is a hollow victory to win at something and still not be satisfied. Success he learned is what you perceive it to be. Everyone who knew and worked with Kevin noticed this change. They all became much more comfortable being around him and even began to enjoy his company. Kevin learned to enjoy what he had earned in life. He and his family were much happier as a result.

WEW means finding ways to position yourself in life so that either way, you win. Using a sales example, if the question is "Would you like to pay for it by check or credit card?" you obviously are going to get the sale regardless of the answer. Often, when we are faced with difficult choices, we feel that we are faced with a problem. However, choices should not be perceived as problems. They are opportunities that often can lead to success, no matter what our ultimate decisions might be.

Finding ways to make either choice the winning one is ultimately the goal of learning to lead your life with a WEW attitude.

Sometimes, we see choices as problems. We worry about making the right decision, when, in reality, either would be a good one. We worry about choosing the red car or the blue car, whether to have fish or chicken for dinner, or to accept offer A or offer B. People often expend great energy worrying about things that a WEW attitude or life's philosophy would keep them from fretting over so much. In the end, it is not so much the choice you make, but what you make of the choice. If you spend the whole dinner wishing that you had selected the fish instead of the chicken, you will enjoy the meal that much less. The same is true for the major decisions you make in life.

Thinking in terms of superlatives can be a problem. It does not have to be a winner-take-all situation, and you do not have to be a superstar to be successful. It is not always an all-or-nothing situation. Other players on the team also have rewarding and successful careers, often with much more personal satisfaction from playing the sport than the star player. You need to avoid falling into this superstar model view of success. There is enough success available for everyone to reach his or her goals. Managing expectations, both yours and of key others, in your life can greatly affect your ability to find winning solutions in just about any situation. Winning truly is a state of mind.

The Negotiating Life Strategies Model

The following model puts into perspective the differences between what we *want* in life and what we *need*, as well as the differences between what we *earn* and *negotiate* in life. Let's look first at the need/want continuum.

Need/Want Continuum

The need/want continuum makes the distinction between our expectations versus our desires. These are two different concepts although we do not always perceive them as such.

Sometimes logic versus emotion distinguishes these concepts. We may more logically pursue the things that we need in life and more emotionally pursue that which we want. Think about what dictates your decision making. What should be the dominant way of thinking? As we further explore this model, you will get a better idea of your predominant way of arriving at decisions.

Getting what we either need or want is always complex and driven by both logical and emotional motivations. In either case, a number of factors will determine our success in pursuit of what we either need or want in life.

Getting What You Need/Want Factors

Desire—how badly we need or want something plays a major role in the success of achieving the goal. Some people are hugely motivated to reach their goals in life. Nothing, it seems, can stop achievement of their objectives. Desire is a powerful driver and can overcome many potential obstacles.

Determination—similar to desire but different in the sense that this factor is what sustains desire over the longer term. Determination is what keeps a person's desire alive. It is easy to be passionate about a goal for a short time but much more difficult over the longer haul. This is when the determination factor makes a difference.

Direction—the direction we go in pursuit of what we want is important to our success in achieving our objectives. Heading in the right direction, or not, towards our goals is of paramount importance. Direction can be a difficult concept to grasp for many. Too often people pursue goals in the wrong direction. Their lack of direction is usually readily apparent to others but not themselves. You see people pursuing dreams in illogical directions. Although going down the road not taken conventionally may prove to be the path to success, often it is not. We need to find the best directions to go in pursuit of our dreams and sometimes need guidance to find our way.

Decisions—your life is sum of the decisions you make, both good and bad. Each decision takes you down a different path or direction. Making the best decisions to get where you want to go is critically important to getting what you both want and need in life. Most decisions once made cannot be undone. We live with our decisions. We hope that we learn from our past decisions to help us make better decisions in the future.

Earn/Negotiate Continuum

The Earn/Negotiate continuum looks at what we get in life from a different perspective. This is the results-oriented part of the model. We typically get what we want in two ways—we *earn* it or we *negotiate* it. Here is the distinction. What we earn is what we work for. The classic example is the paycheck we receive for working at our jobs. This is really the sure bet way of getting what we want. We take a great deal of pride and personal satisfaction from our work and rightfully so. Our work helps define who we are as well as provides for us economically. Few people are truly successful in life without earning their way in the world.

However, we also get what we want through negotiations. This is often the differential between getting the minimum or the maximum out of life. Often there are certain limitations concerning what we can earn in our lifetimes. Our earning power is usually determined by external factors such as our employer's pay policies or scale, the number of hours or even years that we can work during our careers, the market conditions in the field of work we pursue, etc. However, there are no such limits on what we might be able to negotiate in life.

Negotiation in this sense is more than the simple concept of debating over the price or conditions of a deal that we might make. Negotiation as used in this model represents what we get in life other than what we earn. You can negotiate virtually anything in life. Negotiate in this sense is not limited to the classic example of parties making proposals to one another until an agreement is reached. A negotiation in this sense represents anything that is obtained or gained in a manner other than working or earning it by working. Negotiation may be profits made from a purchase, a stock market investment that pays off, a successful business venture, etc. In other words, negotiation for purposes of this model is any way that you can significantly move ahead towards reaching your financial and personal goals in life not limited by simply earning a paycheck.

The Difference Between Earn and Negotiate

The difference between earn and negotiate is often a matter of discovering what options are available. People do not always take advantage of all the options they have available to them. Sometimes, we tend to take the default option, as it often is the path of least resistance. In terms of this model, the default would be earning our living. Again, this is not to say that there is anything at all wrong with pursuing this option. And as mentioned previously, earning your living is a not only a virtuous and greatly rewarding part of life, it is also a prerequisite to being in a position to negotiate what we want in life as well. Few successful negotiators have not spent a great portion of their lives working hard to earn their position in life. However, there typically are many more options available to us, most of which we may not even know about or even imagine. Those who are most successful also typically dream the biggest and in

Technicolor™. They are *possibility* thinkers. They spend far less time thinking about reasons why something cannot happen than thinking about how to make it happen. They find out exactly what options might exist before making decisions. Sometimes, there are great opportunities available just for the asking.

Understanding the Negotiation Life Strategies Model

Let's look at these two continuums presented in a model. This model helps us better understand the intersection between these concepts and their relationship to one another. The model also helps us better understand our own philosophy and perspectives concerning achieving our goals and even our dreams.

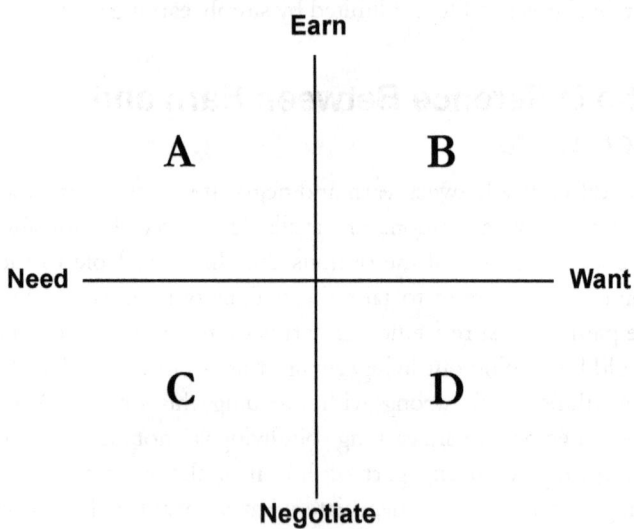

Let's begin at the top of the model with *Earn*. As mentioned, most people need to earn what they get in life typically by hard work, usually in the employ of others. This is both honorable and hopefully satisfying. However, the model begins to look beyond the basic concept of work. It begins to explore the motivation for working in terms of what we are trying to accomplish through employment. The most basic objective is to earn what we need to support our families and ourselves. This is what makes the economic cycles of work operate. We work to provide goods and services for others who also work to purchase the goods and services they need, and so the cycle continues. This is represented by quadrant A in the model.

However, some people work harder and perhaps smarter and are able to earn more than just what they *need* but also what they *want*. This represents quadrant B in the model. In reality, most people are motivated to earn in life both what they need and what they want. We spend our lives living in both quadrants A and B of this model. For some, the pursuit of quadrant B is overwhelming. This is becoming more and more of a problem in our society today.

Some say that we have become a society of overachievers who work tirelessly to fulfill our dreams for a more expensive lifestyle than previous generations experienced. Looking in retrospect, our parents and grandparents may have struggled financially just to put a roof overhead and food on the table—things we take for granted today. We, as a society today, are more focused on purchasing the latest technology in home entertainment or the most prestigious automobile that we can borrow enough money to buy. This balance between earning what we need and what we want is obviously influenced by the economic resources that we are able to earn in our lifetime. Some professions allow incumbents in those jobs to spend more of their income and resources on quadrant B things. Others force people to remain more focused on quadrant A. Unfortunately, there are also those who cannot afford to be even in quadrant A.

Depending on your perspective, each of these quadrants would look like something worth aspiring to if you have not achieved the next level. From the outside, just being able to afford to pay for what you need in life would look very inviting. The same is true for being able to afford what you want to obtain in life.

Next, let's look at the bottom of the model—*negotiate*. There are certain things in life that you might be able to negotiate both from a need and want perspective. Great financial wealth is more likely a result of negotiation than earning. Investments are a negotiation in actuality. You negotiate by risking your money in hopes of a return on the investment. In principle at least, the more you invest or negotiate, the greater the potential return or possible loss. Negotiating the best investments yields the greatest return or creation of wealth. However, as mentioned in the beginning chapters, we negotiate for even the smallest of things sometimes. We may negotiate for what we need in life. Going into the boss's office and asking for a raise because you believe that you are being underpaid is a negotiation. You are implying perhaps subtly, or not so subtly, that if you do not get the raise, you will leave the organization. Dickering over the price of a new car or home is an example of negotiating for what you need in life; that is unless you are purchasing an estate or an expensive car, and then you would be negotiating for something you want.

There are individuals who may rely almost exclusively on negotiating what they need in life. They may be people who live their lives dependent on the earnings of others for any number of reasons, including those that are legitimately acceptable. There are also those who may try to negotiate their basic needs by taking advantage of those who have earned their way in life. These individuals may or may not always be negatively judged by their strategy towards getting what they need and want in life. Finding what might be considered negotiating your way through life might be considered an enviable lifestyle for many. It is relatively easier to make it in life by working for a living. What is difficult is to make it in life without working. Typically, we lead our lives through a combination of strategies that could fall into all four quadrants of the model.

Finding the right balance between these various strategies can help you better achieve your goals and find *Winning Either Way*.

Winning Expectations

To understand the concepts of *Winning Either Way*, you may need to change your expectations. The problem with most people's mindsets about getting what they want is that they have an all-or-nothing attitude. They cannot always see that there may be positives in just about any situation. There may be hidden value in many situations that you need to discover or uncover. Like the old saying, there is always a silver lining in every cloud. This is not to say that you should lower your expectations or standards in life but that you need look at things differently. To do this, you may need to better understand the "what's in it for me" in many situations. Sometimes the "what's in it for me" is not obvious when a desired goal is not achieved. You may not get what you originally set out to achieve but may find something of value, perhaps even greater value, than you first sought. Often, what we learn from what we might initially consider an unsuccessful effort is of the greatest value.

To illustrate this last point, think about what happens when attempts to be successful fail. Sometimes, unsuccessful efforts are the turning points in a person's life. What can be learned from failure is more valuable than what you might learn from success. We learn from failure for a number of reasons. First, failure is typically an emotional event for most people. It has an impact on us. It causes us to feel strong emotions; it gets our attention. This is the good news. Failure should have this kind of effect on us. If not, we might become apathetic and begin to accept failure. Failure should be a motivator to change. Failure should tell us to try something different next time. Insanity, it is said, is to keep doing the same thing and expecting different results.

The most important thing is not to give up. Failure should be viewed as a learning opportunity. It is another chance to get it right the next time. Failure is part of everyone's learning curve. The next time you try to do something, you will have the benefit from what you learned from failing the last time. That is, if you learn the lessons that failure provides.

For example, any successful salesperson will tell you that you will not make every sale you attempt to make. If you are going to pursue a career in sales, you need to learn to deal with failure. A salesperson must approach each potential customer with confidence that he or she will buy the product or service. Failure to sell to the last prospective customer cannot diminish the salesperson's confidence that he or she will be successful with the next potential customer. If a salesperson gets into a self-defeatist attitude due to lack of success selling to past prospects, he or she might as well give it up. The salesperson will talk his or herself out of each potential sale. No need to worry about the competition in this circumstance, for the salesperson will become the competition.

Experienced salespersons learn that you need to maximize every potential sales situation, even those in which you may not be successful in making the sale. Other goals that might be accomplished could lead to other sales. For instance, the salesperson might ask for and receive a lead from the prospective customer that could result in a future sale. Alternatively, the salesperson might just make a positive impression on the customer that enhances his or her reputation for a future sale.

Getting What You Really Want in Life

The salesperson might ask for feedback that could help his or her make a better sales presentation in the future. Whatever the case, the salesperson tries to leave the prospective customer in a positive way. It might be simply handing out a business card or product or service brochure but the presentation ends on a positive note. The effective salesperson's creed is if you cannot make a sale, make a friend. By following this approach, the salesperson is maximizing the opportunity to make a future sale, perhaps even bigger than the potential of the one that got away.

> *Tyler Carlson was one of the company's top salespersons. In just a little over a year, somehow he was able to set sales records never before achieved by any salesperson previously. He was so good that the company would send him into sales territories where others had previously not been successful and he would somehow establish a customer base. How he did this was a question that was on the mind of many of his peers who were constantly being shown up by Tyler's amazing sales record. The management of the company also wanted to know how he did it, so others could learn his sales techniques. Many thought that his success was simply a result of his outgoing personality or some other personal characteristic that Tyler possessed. However, Tyler really did not have significantly better personal skills or more charisma than any of the other salespersons working for the company had.*
>
> *The secret of Tyler's sales success was simply this—he ensured that something positive came out of every sales call he made, even if it did not result in a sale. His philosophy was if he could make a sale, he should try to make a positive connection with the potential customer. He would even stay in touch with potential customers to whom he had previously made his sales presentation to make sure that their needs had not changed. He worked hard to build a relationship with these contacts and provided whatever*

> *services he could offer to them, such as price quotes, competitive bids, or other information that they might ask of him, free of charge. He learned about their businesses by doing research that often only required a simple internet search, and he would often make suggestions about how to improve their business. He did not try to sell them products or services that they really did not need. He would try to find the most economical way that their needs could be met by the company's products and services, even if it cost him potential sales. He studied the competition and knew their products and services well. He did not try to downgrade the competition if they did not deserve it and acknowledged when they had a superior product. He would be honest with customers if a competitor's product might serve their needs better and even advise them as to which competitor's product would be the best buy for their needs. However, despite Tyler's endorsement of competitor's products, these customers more often than not still bought from him.*

The key is in understanding that the true value that exists in any situation might not always be apparent at first. Expectations play a big part in the process. A successful negotiation is as much attitude as it is anything else. Failure is a negotiable item—one for which you set the parameters and define. The successful salesperson does not consider a sales presentation that does not result in a sale necessarily as a failure but rather as an opportunity that has not yet come to fruition. As did Tyler in the previous story, the successful salesperson seeks the positive in the interaction and maximizes the chances of winning in the future in the form of making a sale.

Winning is a realistic objective if you look at it objectively. It is more a state of mind than it is anything else. Often, we fall into the syndrome of "yes or mad." Yes or mad means that if we do not get the answer we want, then we get upset and sometimes do things that are more self-destructive than constructive towards reaching our goals. A much better approach would be not to invest our energies and emotions on the prospect of failure but rather on what is necessary to win the next time. Every situation should be looked at as a learning experience. Learn from it and move on.

The rewards in life come in many different forms. You need to establish your own reward system. You can reinforce yourself and your efforts in many different ways. *Self-talk* is important. Self-talk is what you say to yourself, even if it is only in your thoughts. If you fill your head with negative thoughts and concepts, that is how you will likely behave. If a salesperson approached a potential customer with a negative attitude, what do you think his or her chances would be of making a sale? You need to set the tone for your life yourself. You need to control what you have control over—yourself. No one else can do this for you. You need to establish personal rewards for your own behavior. You can buy yourself something or just reinforce yourself for being the way you want to be. You choose; after all, it is your life.

New models appear to be emerging today concerning these reward zones for personal success. Today's generation seems to be looking for something else. They seem focused more on instant gratification than on waiting a lifetime to reap the rewards that life potentially has to offer. Will they get it? Who knows—the models for success in life are constantly changing and evolving. Maybe it is realistic to want success without a lifetime of sacrifice and hard work. There may be opportunities in the future that we cannot even fathom today. Winning may take on an entirely new meaning for future generations and they may indeed understand how to achieve this objective in any situation. Regardless, future generations will travel along a new information superhighway that will lead them to destinations we may not even be able to envision.

The Future Redefined

Children love to ask their parents in the first few minutes of a long car trip, "Are we there yet?" This question may be difficult, if not impossible, ever to answer. We indeed will never "get there" when it comes to arriving to the future. The future and what it brings will constantly be slipping ahead, just slightly out of our grasp. Future generations will continue to try to visualize what the next changes will be. Even with all of the advancements and new tools they will have to work with that we cannot even conceptualize today, they may be no more accurate in their predictions. And so it goes, each generation trying to understand what the next might be like. However, they might find that as lessons we learn from our history books, some things never really do change. Thankfully, human nature will always offer some constants in the midst of all this future change ahead. As complex as human beings are, our human nature does not really change that much. Human characteristics such as greed, love, hate, envy, etc. have been around as long as man has existed and undoubtedly will be for as long as our race continues. Maybe this is why we are the way we are—to keep some things predictable throughout the generations of humankind.

The following are just a few of the possibilities that the future may hold:

Computer Bosses

The computer will be the ultimate boss in the future. You may be working for a massive microchip, a computer program, someday... "Boy, the computer was a real tyrant today," a future working person may commiserate to his or her significant other at the end of the workday. "I don't think that this system likes me very much. I know that it has been giving all the good assignments to Joe who just started on this network. He's such a suck-up (there will still be such people in the future), always feeding the computer new data all the time. He doesn't think

Getting What You Really Want in Life

I know what's he's been up to but I've seen him sneaking data input into the computer."

Redefining the Workplace

The likely future workplace will be working on-line from your home computer system. We will have virtual workplace with no buildings or physical property except computer and telecommunications equipment. All meetings will be teleconferenced. Employees will be working remotely from home or a central transmittal center as part of organizational website systems. Most commercial buildings will be replaced by computer data banks. Commuting to work will become almost extinct in the future. Traffic congestion will be on the information superhighway, not the thruway. Business casual will be your bathrobe and slippers. A completely new clothing line will appear called Business Loungewear—pajamas you can work in. Executives will wear wing-tipped bedroom slippers and have pinstriped pajamas with company logos on their bathrobes. Virtual reality at work—commuting simulators to make you feel you have driven to work in the morning equipped with construction delays. These simulators will put you in the right mind frame (frustrated and angry) when you begin working.

Shared Net User Groups or SNUGS

Future generations will work in Shared Net User Groups or SNUGS who will have access to a common data base that provide all of the information they need in their daily personal and work lives. These SNUGS will become like virtual communities much like a small town. The future version of a job transfer or change might involve being moved to a different access group or website. This can be very traumatic, as much as being physically transferred. The family moves their data access as well. There will be tearful good-byes to chat room buddies lists even though you may never actually meet. People will ask not to be virtually transferred until teenage children graduate from their virtual Home High School.

Career/Life Total Integration

Where careers and personal lives begin and end will become far less distinct. The entire family unit will become more involved in the parent(s) careers. Your e-mail address on the information superhighway will become more important than your street address where you live. The future will create ways of getting messages to you that are even more obtrusive. There will be no escape. The Dick Tracy wristwatch—a tiny, complete computerized communications device capable of sending and receiving messages anyplace, anytime—will become an unfortunate reality. Everyone will wear one. It will be a great aid to the elderly. "I've fallen off-line and can't get back on the system," will be a common message to emergency Network Emergency Response workers from this growing segment of our population.

Return to Home-Centered Lifestyles

History once again will repeat itself, as it will be like going back to an agrarian society of sorts. Only in the future, the cash crop will be information. Future societies will become more home-centered, both physically and intellectually connected to the rest of the world. Future homes will be designed with this lifestyle in mind. Home information centers will include host computers that control everything in the home. Today, we have redundant independent systems— TV, VCR, doorbells, telephones, TV cable, telephone lines, computerized microwaves and ovens, thermostats, cell phones, etc. In the future, these will all be combined into one central system.

Home computers will take over many of the parenting responsibilities, such as daycare, while parents work. Sensors activated by toxic smells or moisture content in the room will tell you when to change diapers. Employment terminations will be simply a denial of password access into the network. Without that, you are finished.

Future Cars

If you do have to leave your home for some reason, an Automated Response Tracking (ART) system will control the drive in your Hydrogen Powered Transport Unit (HPTU). Traffic accidents will be programmed out of existence. Our future cars will become smarter than we are. "Didn't you mean to take a left at that light?" ART will inquire as you try to fake out the system as you head for the golf course (virtual) instead of staying home and working on that report due next Tuesday. "Mr. Johnson is going to be very upset with you. He was expecting that report to be completed on time," ART warns you as you pull into the clubhouse parking lot and begin to get your Golf Game Virtual Experience (GGVE) computer program out of the car. "I'm afraid that I'm going to have to report this behavior to Mr. Johnson. It's part of my programming." You begrudgingly shove your GGVE back in its compartment and head back home to work on Mr. Johnson's project due next Tuesday.

The future will be redefine winning as the "rules of the game" change and evolve. Your ability to adapt to these changes may become the most important factor in determining how satisfied you feel about getting what you really want in the future.

Life Strategy Questions

- Are you getting what you really want in life? If your answer is anything but "yes," should you reconsider your life strategy for reaching your goals?

- Looking back at the Life Strategy Model introduced in this chapter, should you change your approach to getting what you want?

- Are you settling for something less than what you really want in life? If so, how can you change this situation?

- How can setting different goals for yourself help change the outcomes you achieve?

- Are you over relying on a particular approach or philosophy for getting what you want in your life?

- How could utilizing a number of different approaches to achieving your goals help ensure you reach these objectives?

CHAPTER 3

Taking Charge of Your Life

J ust how much of what you worry about in your life actually happens? In reality, about 80 percent of what we worry about never occurs. In other words, we might spend the majority of our lives fretting about things that will never actually happen. That is a lot of unnecessary stress and anxiety in our lives for nothing. The point is that we often worry about things that really are not that important in the bigger scheme of things in life.

Try an experiment about worrying. Record what you worry about for the next week and compare these worries to what really happened. Let's call this your "Worry Log." An example of such a log is presented below. At the end of the week, compare the number of "yes" versus "no" entries you make in the last column of this Worry Log. You will be amazed how much time you actually spend worrying about things that never happen. Sometimes, even when things you worry about do come true, the results are not always as bad as we imagined. Think about those "blessings in disguise" that have happened in your life. There are times and circumstances when the worst thing that could happen turn out to be the best thing that could have happened. Things have a way of often turning out for the best. Life is often unpredictable in this manner. Remembering that this is always possible can lessen the stress and anxiety we often experience worrying about things that never come to fruition.

Worry Log

Things you worried about *List each separately.*	What was the outcome?	Did you worry about this unnecessarily? *Yes/No*

Winning Either Way is about taking charge of your life. Part of doing this is to focus on things that you can have an impact upon and stop worrying about that which you cannot. You may find that you waste so much of your time and energies on things that never actually happen. You can control what you think about and focus your attention and energies. These thoughts and energies should be centered on getting what you want in life, not worrying about things that will most likely never occur. Just think about all the energy that you may waste every moment you worry about things about which you cannot really do much or anything. Refocusing this energy can have a tremendous impact on your life.

Overcoming Victim Mentality

Victim mentality is the syndrome in which individuals feel that other people or circumstances in life are controlling their lives. They feel they are actually victims of these outside forces with little or no control over what happens to them. In reality, others may victimize some people. There are over controlling bosses, spouses, family members, friends, etc. that may be dominant forces in people's lives. However, even in these situations, there are still choices that people make that allow this victimization to exist. Part of taking control of your life is to break free of any victim mentality that you may feel. If this is the case, you need to take control of your life and stop blaming others for your problems or frustrations.

Let's go back to the Life Strategies Hierarchy introduced in the last chapter. People suffering from victim mentality are probably living their lives at the lower levels of this model, likely stuck in default or concession behaviors. They feel caught in a trap with the same cycle of frustrations facing them every day. What someone in this situation needs to do is to look at ways to break free of this syndrome. The challenge is to change the way you approach the challenges you face in life. The first step is to stop blaming others and do what you need to do to break free of being a victim. You have choices you can make but you need to make sure that you make good ones. You do not want to make matters worse by making bad choices that will only aggravate the situation or dilemma in which you feel you are. You can make better choices by thinking strategically about the possible outcomes of your decisions. Often just giving some concentrated thought about what these possibilities may be will help lead you to better decisions that are more thoughtful and will lead to much better results. The following model will help you better envision the outcome of your decisions:

Beyond What Comes Our Way

Too many people simply accept what comes their way in life. This is the classic default mentality. This is fine as long as you are satisfied with settling for the default that life may present to you. If not, then you need to do something about it. The following continuum describes our satisfaction index concerning our life expectations:

What we want	→	What we get	→	What we expect	→	What we accept	→	What we think we deserve

It is possible for all of these "Whats" to be consistent with one another and moving in the same direction as shown above. In other words, what we want, get, expect, accept, and feel we deserve can be all aligned. If this is the case, we should be happy and content with life. Hopefully, that will be the case for you. However, it is possible and even probable that all of these "Whats" are not in alignment in your life. The greater the inconsistency, the greater a person's dissatisfaction may be with what they are getting out of life. Let's look at these "Whats" in more detail.

What We Want

Thinking about we want in life is important. We need to have goals, even dreams, that we want to achieve in life. Knowing what you want can help provide you with direction and guidance towards achieving your goals. Without goals, you may have no real direction in life. Set clear goals for yourself and do not be limited in your dreams.

What We Get

What we get is often directly related to what we want. Like the old saying, "if you don't ask for it, you will never get it." Again, many things in life are there for the asking, but we also must be careful what we ask for because we might just get it. Some things require us to do certain things to earn or obtain these goals but they are achievable. Other things require great effort, skill, resources, or even luck to get. Regardless, few things will just fall into our laps without our setting goals to achieve them and then doing whatever is necessary to obtain them.

What We Expect

Another saying goes, "You get what you expect in life." Often, our expectations create results. Our attitude towards achieving our goals has a great deal to do with our success in achieving these goals. If you do not pursue a goal aggressively, the chances of success will be far less. Even worse, would be to have a defeatist attitude. In this sense, we often defeat ourselves because of our expectations or lack of positive expectations. Changing your expectations can significantly impact the ultimate outcome. We need to expect success both in attitude and in our actions. Confidence is the first positive step towards success. Learn to expect success.

What We Accept

Different people will accept different things in life. Our personal standards have a great deal to do with what we might be willing to accept in life. *Winning Either Way* has a lot to do with this very concept. Sometimes learning to accept what you have in life and even be grateful for these things is a good thing. Too often, people spend their lives pursuing bigger and bigger goals never even enjoying anything they accomplish. The quest or even obsession in achieving the next level is all that is important. There needs to be a balance between establishing high standards for yourself and enjoying the rewards that life has presented you by either earning or negotiating these things.

What We Think We Deserve

This perhaps is the most telling of all the steps. This is where the satisfaction quotient in life really exists. If we think that we have achieved what we truly deserve, the chances of contentment or happiness will be greater. If not, watch out. There are few emotions stronger than one's feeling that they have been cheated out of something desired in life, particularly if this is a strong or important desire in life. *Winning Either Way* is also about reconciling this factor if it is a problem for you. Too many people carry huge chips on their shoulders because they feel that life has cheated or ripped them off in some way. You need to rid yourself of this burden if you are carrying it around with you. Lighten your load and get rid of these feelings. Wipe the slate clean and set new expectations based on where you are today. You will ultimately feel better and have a better chance of happiness in the future.

Who Is in Charge of Your Life?

The short answer to the above question is that **you** are in charge of your life. To many, it may not really seem that way. Life's situations can make people feel under the control of others, and, to some extent, this may be true. There will always be people that we are accountable to or to whose wishes we need to comply. However, this does not mean that you do not still have choices. We are free to make choices and decisions but we must also understand the possible consequences of such decisions. Our lives are essentially a result of the decisions we make in life, both good and bad. How we got to where we are in life at this very moment is sum of all of the decisions we have previously made in our lives or which possibly have been made for us.

We start out in life with others making virtually all of the decisions in our life. As we grow older, we begin to make more and more of our life's decisions until we are able to make all of these decisions. Your parents at some point in your life may have wanted you to do or become something that you may or may not have wanted to do. They may have hoped or even planned that you would pursue a certain profession or business. Before you were in control of the decisions in your life, you may have complied with these wishes. You may have studied what you were expected to in school and perhaps even entered into a profession or business because of other's desires, but at some point in your life, you need to decide for yourself. Only you can make the decisions that make you happiest. The only way to be truly successful in life is to be what you want to be. Anything less would be a compromise or, even worse, a default.

So, how did you get to where you are today? What were those critical decisions that were made that led you to where you are at this precise moment? Thinking about where you have been can help you better understand where you may be heading. Think about your *life's journeys* to date. Are you satisfied or happy with the journey so far? If not, where would you have liked your life journey to take you? Perhaps even more importantly are you happy with where your life journey is headed? If not, what can you do to change the direction of your journey? What can you control in your life that can change the course of your life?

Think about those critical moments, events, and decisions in your life that lead you to this moment in time. If you had to replay some of them, what would you have done differently? Has a pattern in your life led you to where you are today? Does this pattern still exist in your life today? Are there certain influencers that play an important role in your life's decisions today?

Your Life's Strategy

The point in exploring these and similar questions is to identify your *life's strategy*. Negotiating your life's strategy is the topic of a later chapter of this book, but for now, let's identify what this strategy might be. Your life's strategy may be very clear to you. You may have given it a great deal of thought, although you probably did not think of it in these terms. Having a clear and definite life strategy is important to our happiness. Without such a strategy, we may not have the direction we need to take us on the life journey we really want to pursue. Without a life strategy, we may be forced to the default options in life. Again, this is fine if you are going to be satisfied with someone else making these options or decisions for you. But if you truly want to be in control of your life, you need to develop a strategy that you are going to follow or, at least, attempt to follow. Again, you may not always reach your destinations but at least you will be headed in the directions of your goals and even dreams in life. This is not a bad path to follow.

The Self-fulfilling Prophecy

A prophecy is a premonition, an insight, a foretelling. A self-fulfilling prophecy is one in which you predict things about and for yourself and do things to make them come true. A self-fulfilling prophecy can be both positive and negative. Often, people unwittingly create these negative self-fulfilling prophecies when, in actuality, they are the last thing they want to have happen to them. In this sense, the fear that something will happen to them actually causes it to come to fruition.

Here is a simple example. You are invited to a party that you really do not want to attend but feel compelled to accept the invitation. Maybe you do not know many of the people who will be there, you think you will feel out of place, or you do not like someone who you know is going to be there. You spend the weeks before the event dreading going, particularly so, as the date of the party approaches. You keep telling yourself how miserable you are going to be at this party and keep replaying in your head how much you will hate attending. How much would you expect to enjoy yourself when you arrive at this party? Obviously, with this much negative anticipation, and even dread, you probably would not enjoy yourself at all at the party. This would be an example of a negative self-fulfilling prophecy. You actually contribute to something happening by how you anticipate it in advance. In this example, going to a party convinced that you will not enjoy yourself will almost certainly ensure that this result will occur.

However, the reverse can also occur. A self-fulfilling prophecy can also be positive. Having a positive attitude can also create success. Think again about the salesperson in the previous story that approaches each customer with the attitude that they will buy something compared to the salesperson who does just the opposite. Who do you believe will be the most successful? Surely, the salesperson that approached every customer as a buyer will be. So much of being successful is about attitude.

Winning Either Way

A successful attitude can greatly change the outcome even in situations where success is unlikely. Filling your head with negative thoughts or doubts will make being successful less likely. You will defeat yourself before you even begin. Sports psychologists clearly understand this concept. They teach athletes to focus on being successful by creating mental images of performing their sport flawlessly. They help athletes envision what it would be like to hit that homerun, run for a touchdown, or sink that long putt.

A professional golfer was once asked during a televised interview about his play during a major championship tournament after he completed his third round. The sportscaster asked him about one particularly poor drive he had made on the last hole. The golfer said he did not remember much about that poor shot. The not very astute sportscaster insisted on trying to get the golfer to discuss the poor shot. After several unsuccessful prompts, the sportscaster finally gave up and asked him about a critical birdie putt he had made on the ninth hole. The golfer responded to this question with great enthusiasm and went into considerable detail about the putt.

The point is that the golfer was not about to focus on what he had done poorly during the round but rather on what he had done well. He did not want to begin the last day of the tournament with his head filled with self-doubts and lack of confidence in his abilities. He had proven to himself that he was capable of good and even outstanding golf and that is what he was going to expect of himself during his final round.

Avoiding a self-destructive strategy is not only important for professional athletes but for ordinary people as well. Focusing on that which you can control rather than on that which you cannot is the key. It does not do an athlete much good to complain about the playing conditions that might exist that might adversely affect his or her performance. He or she cannot do anything about this factor. Just complaining about it will not do them much good. More productive would be to think about what adjustments or strategy for play must be made to adjust to the current playing conditions. In life, we are often confronted with different or even adverse conditions that we must deal with in order to do the things we need to do. We often need to adjust our strategy to compensate for changing conditions. Sticking with a particular plan or strategy despite changes in the playing field of life may ultimately turn out to be a poor strategy. Adapting to these changes and having the flexibility to change your direction and course in life is critically important to learning to deal effectively in most or all situations.

Influencing Skills

Think about just how much influence you have concerning what happens to you. How much can you influence others that are an important part of your life? How could improving or increasing your influence impact your life? You do not have to be in a position of authority necessarily to have an influence over others or yourself for that matter. It all depends on your sphere of influence. Your sphere of influence is that which you can control either directly or indirectly. Some things you have a direct influence over, others you can only have an indirect impact upon, and some things you do not have any control over. Understanding these differences is important. People often greatly underestimate their sphere of influence on all three of these factors. Here are the differences between these three levels of influence:

Direct Influence

The first thing to understand about your level of influence is that the only thing you can truly control in your life is yourself. You are in complete charge of your behaviors. Some people are in constant denial of this fact but it is true. They blame others for their behaviors. In this sense, they truly suffer from victim mentality. A true victim is someone who is under the control of someone else. This is paramount to being in a self-imposed mental and emotional jail. They allow others to dictate how they are expected to behave or even think. This is particularly tragic if someone else determines his or her self-concept.

If you truly want to take control of your life, you need to be the one who influences your thoughts, behaviors, and actions. You choose how you should and will respond, not other people. As an adult, you should make your own decisions, including how you will respond and behave. This is not to say that you should not listen to and respect the opinions of those important others in your life. This is part of a good decision-making process. Why would you not consider the advice and opinions of those who have more life experience and expertise than you do have? That certainly would not be wise, but you need to recognize that even the most influential people in your life should only be indirect influencers. You still need to be in charge. You need to make the final decision based upon your own values, beliefs, information, intuitions, and advice from others. To do anything less is abdication of your direct influence over yourself.

Indirect Influencers

"What am I supposed to do about it?"

"That's not my job."

"I am not responsible for that."

"It wasn't my fault."

These are all things that you frequently hear people say, trying to absolve them of responsibility. We often find ourselves playing the blame game. We blame other people, circumstances, institutions, governments, etc. All of these behaviors are attempts to deny that we can have an influence over these things. It is easier to blame someone or something else than to take responsibility. However, if you study the most successful people, you will find that they are less interested in playing the blame game. There is little to be gained in this game.

Sitting around blaming others for what you are dissatisfied with will do little and probably nothing to improve the situation. This is really just a lot of wasted energy. Instead, you need to do whatever you can to try to change things. You may not be able to have a direct impact but you still may be able to influence. For example, if you do not like the rules, get involved in trying to change them. Make your opinions heard in a manner that is acceptable and respectful. Find out what mechanisms there are in the system for changing things and get involved. Talk to people about what you think needs to be done and be willing to be part of the solution, not just a critic of the problem. The greater you enlarge your sphere of influence in this matter, the more control you have over your life.

No Influence

Unquestionably, there are things in life that you have no influence over. We have to accept these things for what they are and move on in life. Obsessing or even worrying about things that you cannot influence is an exercise in futility. The trick is in understanding the difference or distinction between those things that you can influence and those, which you cannot. There may be a fine line between the two.

For example, say that you are planning an outside event such as a wedding reception, graduation or birthday party or whatever. The major factor that you cannot control will be the weather. No matter how many times you check with the National Weather Service, you cannot change that impending storm heading your way during the very time of your planned outdoor event. However, you can have a rain contingency plan. You could establish a rain date or arrange for an inside venue. You may not be able to influence the weather, but you can make plans in case it does not cooperate. You can almost always do more about a situation than you may initially believe is possible if you give it some thought and do some planning. In this sense, you can extend your sphere of influence even in situations that you think you have little or no control.

Institutionalized Thinking

Have you ever thought about why you think about things the way you do? We all have opinions on many or most things that we encounter during our daily lives. We typically give little or no thought about why we think or believe the way we do about most things. We do this unconsciously and for the most part, it is of little concern why we feel about something compared to how we feel about it. We typically have strong feelings about our beliefs, particularly those that we feel define who we are.

However, many of our beliefs may be things that have become *institutionalized*. Institutionalized thinking is basing our opinions more on the way we may have been taught to think about something rather than on our true beliefs. It simply is something that occurs in life—not necessarily a bad thing. We are taught many of our beliefs at home, as we grow up. We may be a Republican or Democrat based on our parents' political beliefs. Our educational institutions greatly influence our beliefs and teach us how to think about many different subjects. People we associate with often help shape many of our beliefs. Our careers also contribute greatly to our beliefs often providing us with unique experiences that create and reinforce them. Organizations often issue position statements to influence employees' thinking on certain political or social issues important to their overall business goals or agendas.

Sometimes, it is good to differentiate between what we truly believe and what we are taught or expected to believe about certain things in life. The point is that you have a right to believe anyway that you want. You do not have to adopt the

Taking Charge of Your Life

beliefs of others if you truly believe differently. Part of your sphere of influence needs to be over yourself and your feelings and beliefs.

It truly may not be a good idea to begin questioning or challenging all of your current beliefs. This would likely result in a very confusing state of mind for you. Our beliefs and values provide a point of reference for us that helps us better understand the world around us. How we got to these beliefs is perhaps not as important as that we are comfortable with these beliefs, and our beliefs do not always have to be perfectly aligned with our value systems. In other words, we are all entitled to have some beliefs or even personal values that may at least seem contradictory to each other. This occurrence is likely the result of a learned or institutionalized value or thought that we acquired somewhat unconsciously during our lifetime. However, there may be certain things that you should rethink to make sure that you are really in touch with your true feelings. Some people are total living contradictions of themselves. They say they feel one way but live their lives another way. This confliction can cause a person much stress.

Ask yourself from time to time, "Why do I feel this way?" Do you really feel how you say you do? Part of being credible is being able to say that you really feel the way you say you do, not just how you perceive you are expected to. Your values do need to be consistent in what you say and what you do. Others judge you on this factor. It is called integrity. Your motives should be based on your values, and they too should be consistent. Having credibility with oneself is the highest form of integrity. Being comfortable with who you are is more important than trying to impress others. This is what leads to self-confidence, a clear conscience, and ultimately happiness in life.

Voice of Authority

Who is your "voice of authority"? Whom do you truly listen to and where do you get your information? We can access many sources of information in our daily lives. The very age we live in provides us with virtually unlimited amounts of information that can be accessed instantaneously. The internet, advanced cellular phones, satellite television, and radio, just to name a few, are all revolutionizing communications, so there really is no reason not to be in touch with others. We can stay informed on a constant basis if we choose to. The sources for our information and the people we listen to are also our choices. Make sure that you are getting your information from the right people. Listening to and acting on bad information can have disastrous consequences in life. Many bad decisions are a result of being ill advised. The best decisions are usually those that were reached because of getting good advice from trusted and reliable sources and then processing this information to the point that we are comfortable with the decision. We need to take ownership for our decisions.

Doing just a little research can make the difference between making good decisions and living with the consequences of a poor or even terrible decision. This research does not always have to be extensive. It can be a simple as asking the right people what they think before moving forward with your decision. This type of corroboration is what most successful management teams in business learn to do. They get the input of all of their subject matter experts that they employ. These experts are on the payroll so there is no reason not to capitalize on their expertise and advice. You may not have experts on your payroll but you still have access to informed people on just about any subject. However, you need to ask the right people the right questions.

For instance, you would not (or should not) ask your doctor for legal advice, your tax accountant for medical advice, or your dentist for help filing your income tax. Asking for advice from the unqualified people in other aspects of your life is essentially doing this same thing. People in our lives do not always have titles that validate their expertise in a particular field the same as found in professional careers. This does not make good advice any easier to find. However, there are some obvious pitfalls to avoid. For instance, seeking financial advice from someone who just filed bankruptcy would probably not be a good decision. Similarly, seeking marital advice from someone who was recently divorced may also be a bad idea. Although these people may be able to share with you what these experiences may have been like, they obviously do not know all the answers to avoiding these problems.

Influencers

Hopefully, you seek advice from the right sources. However, sometimes, others influence us indirectly and even perhaps unconsciously. Others influence us for a variety of factors. These influencers include someone's *position, knowledge, reputation,* and *personal characteristics*.

Position

A person's position in life may bring with it significant authority over others. The influence of position is perhaps best understood looking at the military model. Rank, or in other words, one's position, in a military system brings with it a defined level of authority. A soldier's rank is clearly displayed on his or her uniform so there is no question about the level of influence or authority of the soldier. Each higher rank brings with it greater levels of influence and authority. Soldiers are required to show deference and respect for those of superior rank. To do otherwise would result in military discipline or even a court martial.

Although position may not always be so clearly defined in civilian life, it certainly has its influence. Influence in the corporate world, for instance, is based a great deal on the level or position one holds in the company. Obviously, the chief executive officer, or CEO, of the company wields the most influence as everyone else in the organization reports to him or her. Those in higher positions such as vice presidents may also be powerfully influential, being responsible for significant parts of big organizations. They may use their position power to help the organization reach its financial goals or they may use their influence for more personal gains, even illegally causing corporate scandals such as those that have made headline news in recent years. People can be elected or appointed to public positions or positions in government that can yield tremendous power. These types of positions have certainly seen their share of scandals and corruption over the years as well.

Whatever the case, one's position has a great deal to do with how much influence a person has over others. Be it rank, title, or job level, position is a very important part of the order in the world. Without position, the lines of authority would be much less clear. This could result in chaos. People in higher positions may not always be the best ones to make critical decisions but they are the ones that have been charged with the responsibility to make these decisions. In many situations, there is little or no time to debate who should be in charge or to appoint a leader. Leadership by position has already been determined and needs to be followed unless the person in position has proven his or herself incapable of effective leadership.

Position may also be a function of where someone is in life. Family matriarchs lead extended families for generations, having significant influence over the lives of family members throughout their lifetimes. People may also be respected for what they have achieved during their lifetime by virtue of their accomplishments and influence they have earned as a result.

Knowledge

They say that knowledge is power. In our information age, this is becoming truer every day. Unfortunately, position and knowledge are not always synonymous. This is often a source of great frustration to those who have knowledge but not the position to utilize it fully. Without being in the positions to be able to use their knowledge fully, they are forced to sit back and watch less informed individuals do things with which they might disagree. Organizations are full of subject matter experts that for whatever reason have not been able to aspire to higher positions of influence despite the fact that they are the most knowledgeable. This might occur because of personal characteristics, including their lack of ability to influence others, organizational politics, lack of promotional opportunities, or just luck or circumstance.

Influence without knowledge can be a dangerous combination but unfortunately common. People do reach powerfully influential positions without the knowledge needed to meet the requirements and expectations of these roles. Hopefully, they surround themselves with knowledgeable people and listen to their advice.

Reputation

A person's reputation may not only precede them; it may also define them in many ways. Reputations may be earned or bestowed upon people for many different reasons. People do get reputations that they do not deserve. This fact can be both positive and negative. Shedding a poor or bad reputation is possible by a demonstrated change in behavior or actions. Losing a good reputation can occur in the same manner. However, some reputations may be somewhat impossible to rid. Once someone is labeled a certain way, this reputation may follow him or her seemingly forever. Public images or personae are often indelibly etched in people's minds. A movie star may forever be perceived to be a sex symbol in the public's mind even beyond his or her youth or even lifetime. A politician may always be associated with a past alleged scandal despite a career of distinguished public service. Think about how Elvis Presley is remembered and even idolized as a sex symbol even thirty years after his death or Senator Edward Kennedy is remembered for the Chappaquiddick incident that ruined his chances of ever successfully running for president of the United States.

People will respect a person for his or her reputation at least in the short term or unless proven otherwise. Reputations, although greatly influential, do change, often quickly. Trying to rely on one's reputation to influence others may not always be a sound strategy in life. In the final analysis, one's reputation must be earned every day. To expect others to continue to respect one's influence based on the past rather than the present is just too much to expect of others.

Personal Characteristics

One's personal characteristics play a major role in the degree he or she influences others. Some people are just born leaders. They have the leadership characteristics that people just naturally seem to follow. These characteristics might be influenced by their knowledge, expertise, and experience but probably go beyond these factors. These influencing characteristics have more to do with the individual's *leadership charisma*. Leadership charisma is one of those things that are easier to identify when present than to define. For instance, President John F. Kennedy had leadership charisma. Many of the top executives in business or other organizations have this leadership charisma. Some call it executive presence. You just know when you meet some individuals that they have these personal characteristics. It is debatable if this is something that can be taught or acquired. Certainly, countless executive and leadership training programs try to teach these characteristics.

However, you do not have to be the most charismatic leader or executive to have influencing characteristics. You can have an influence over others by virtue of your integrity, personal example, concern, knowledge or commitment, just to name a few influencing characteristics. People will respect you for who you are if they believe that you are sincere and honest in your presentation of yourself and what you stand for.

It is actually the combination of these four factors—position, knowledge, reputation, and personal characteristics—that ultimately determines the influence one has over others. This is called your *influencing index*. People are either stronger or weaker in each of these four factors that combined create one's influencing index. However, strength in one of these factors can compensate for lack of strength in the others.

For example, a person's position may enable him or her to be greatly influential despite weaknesses in the other three factors. Many might say that George W. Bush during his presidency fit into this category of influencers. Others may be respected solely based upon their expertise. The nightly newscast is full of subject matter experts talking about their field of expertise as it relates to a current news item of general interest to the public. For example, a meteorologist may be on the air to discuss a particular weather event that is about to hit a particular area. This person is influential solely based on his or her knowledge about the upcoming weather conditions that will be affecting the viewers' lives in the immediate future. In this same newscast, another expert may be introduced whose expertise in another field may be the basis for his or her ability to influence viewers. In this case, the person's influence may be more a factor of his or her qualifications or credentials in a field. For instance, a famous forensic expert may be interviewed to shed light on an unsolved crime. Viewers are influenced by this person solely based on his or her reputation as an expert on the subject.

Finally, a person's personal characteristics, including physical appearance, voice, body language, confidence, etc., can greatly affect his or her ability to influence others, even in the absence of the other three influencing factors. These individuals are often called natural born leaders. Now think about someone who is strong in all four of these four influencing factors. Suppose that an individual has aspired to a position of influence, is highly knowledgeable, has earned a great reputation, and has strong personal leadership characteristics. How influential do you think this person would be? What kind of leader do you think this person would make? Obviously, someone strong in all four of these factors would be very influential or a great leader.

Think about how you might measure in each of these four influencing factors. What are your strongest influencing factors? Which are your weakest? How can your stronger influencing factors help compensate for your weaker ones? Having a better understanding of how you might be able to influence others can help you better manage your own strengths and weaknesses as an influential person.

How well do you influence others over which you have no real authority? Influencing without the authority of position or rank over others requires greater strength in the influencing factor of *personal characteristics*, particularly if you are dealing with others over whom you have no direct authority. You may often find yourself in this situation. Your ability to influence without authority could make the difference between achieving your goals in life and just settling for something less. There are ways in which you can be more influential over others even when you do not have any authority over them.

Most situations you may find yourself in probably do not involve clear delineations of authority. In these situations, you probably find yourself simply dealing with the influencing factor of *personal characteristics*. Some people have a tendency at least to try to *take charge* in situations such as this. Their personality styles may be more assertive or aggressive, leading them to be naturally more influential. They assert their opinions and give directions or even orders without anyone appointing them as leader. Others may follow for lack of any other direction or reason not to follow. This is fine as long as everyone is satisfied with his or her role and direction that this situation creates. But what if you are not satisfied when finding yourself in this type of situation? What can you do to become more influential?

It is important that you keep this Influencing Model (position, knowledge, reputation, and personal characteristics) in mind. Think about the relative strength of the others you are dealing with concerning these four factors in relation to your own strengths. If, for instance, you are dealing with someone in a position with great authority, you may decide that you may not be able to be very influential—that is, unless that individual has a very low influencing index on one or more the other three factors. You may have more knowledge on a particular subject or possess stronger influencing personal characteristics than that individual and could use these factors to influence others in the situation. Of course, there may be other situations when the person in a position of authority, say a police officer or the CEO of your company, says you need to do something. Obedience may be the best strategy to follow on this occasion.

If someone has more knowledge about the situation, you may find it best to defer to him or her concerning this influencing factor. It would not make sense to do otherwise, but that does not mean that you still may not be able to have some influence in this situation. Perhaps the knowledgeable person does not have strong personal characteristics to use their knowledge to influence others. You may be able to use their knowledge and your stronger influencing personal characteristics to assume a more influential role.

A person's reputation as an expert or knowledgeable person concerning a particular subject or situation may or may not be well deserved. It might be best to defer to this expert's influence in the situation and learn as much as you can from this individual. Again, to do otherwise would not show good judgment or be beneficial to you. You need to know when to defer to others' influence. However, there may be situations when the apparent expert may not actually be so well qualified or knowledgeable. This is not to say that you should be challenging the credentials of everyone who claims to be an expert. Rather you may still be able to be influential even in the presence of those who are reputed to have expertise in a particular subject or skill.

Influencing without authority is something that we all need to do in our lives. Our ability to influence others may be the key to finding ways to find acceptable outcomes to the many different situations we face during our lives. *Winning Either Way* is often dependent on our influencing ability even in situations where we do not have any real authority. You do not always find yourself in an ideal situation in terms of the influencing model in which you score high on all four factors, particularly being in a formal position of authority over others. Often the authority we get is that which we give to ourselves.

Getting Your Voice Heard

Have you ever felt that you could not get into a conversation or had difficulty getting your opinion heard even when you felt you had something very important to say? If you sometimes feel this way, you are not alone. Many of us often have this problem. However, some people are very good at getting their voice heard in just about any situation. Certain communications techniques people do all the time, but may not always be conscious or keenly aware of, help them get their voices heard. Being more conscious or even strategic about utilizing these communications techniques can help you be better able to get your voice heard, particularly in those situations when you feel you have something very important to say and contribute.

Getting your voice heard can be a difficult challenge. There can be a lot of competition to get the attention of those who you would want to hear what you have to say. Giving some thought or even practicing these tips and techniques can help you get your voice heard in even the most challenging situations. Utilizing these techniques at the right time and in the right circumstances will determine how successful you are in getting your voice heard.

Getting your voice heard can be a challenge in many typical work, as well as social, situations. Often, so many people want to contribute to a discussion that getting the attention of others can be difficult at times. Factors such as familiarity of the group, position, role, reputation, etc. are all important contributors to the amount of attention one might get to have his or her voice "heard." Getting the attention of a group comes much easier for some people than it does for others. Much of one's ability to get the attention of others is a function of his or her personality style and characteristics. However, there are certain things that you can do to help ensure that what you have to say is heard by others who need to hear this information. The following are Ten Tips on *Getting Your Voice Heard*:

Ten Tips on *Getting Your Voice Heard*

1. **Strategic interrupting**—Interrupting is usually considered rude or inappropriate. However, there are times when you have to do this in order to get into a discussion or conversation. Strategic interrupting is a better way to interject your voice into the middle of someone else's talking. You need to look for a break or pause in the other person's conversation that will make your interruption less obtrusive or objectionable. This may be at that second when the other person has just finished a point or emphasis before he or she goes on to the

next point. That is your shot to get into the conversation or discussion. But do not be so focused on getting in on the conversation that you do not hear what the other person is saying. If you miss his or her point, you may find yourself being interrupted yourself.

2. **Non-verbal indicators that you are about to speak**—You may not always be conscious of these non-verbal indicators, but they typically telegraph to others that someone is about to speak. These indicators might include such things as hand gestures, changes in a person's physical position, even an expression on one's face. You can consciously utilize these indicators to let others know that you want to get into the discussion or conversation. Make your non-verbal indicators clear and recognizable. However, as with all of these techniques, timing is critical. Do not send out these indicators at moments in a discussion or conversation when they may not be seen or recognized or when it is less likely that the person speaking will yield the discussion to you.

3. **Sound interjections**—People often make certain sounds that indicate that they want to get into the conversation. These sounds often subtly get others attention and create opportunities for the sound maker to speak. These sounds are usually not words or complete words. They might be something that sounds more like "hmmmm" or a questioning word such as "really?" or perhaps a laugh or even a groan. All of these sounds serve the purpose of sending a message to others that you wish to or are about to speak.

4. **Asking for the "floor"**—People ask for the "floor" in a number of different ways. This is done exactly the way it sounds—you ask for the attention of the group or the person to whom you are talking. This is done by saying something such as, "I would like to say something…" or even "May I have the floor?" However, once you have asked

for the floor you need to make sure that you have something to say worthy of asking for everyone's attention.

5. **Timing the flow of the conversation**—Every conversation has a certain cadence or flow. This is determined by the level of participation on the parties involved in the conversation. One person may be determining this flow depending on his or her influence, knowledge, dominance, etc. However, if it is truly a conversation indicating that there is a sharing of "air" time between participants, you will notice that there are certain timing patterns emerging. The dominant person in the conversation will allow others to express themselves at certain points, probably after this individual has made his or her most recent point. This is your best opportunity to join in. If you time your attempt wrong, that is as the dominant speaker is just beginning his or her point or response, you may find it more difficult to get into the conversation.

6. **Appealing to group opinion leaders**—An effective technique is to address directly the conversation opinion leader with a question or even challenge to something that he or she has already said. Most likely, this will result in this individual responding directly to you rather than the others in the conversation. This will give you opportunities to be invited by this dominant person to respond. Be sure that you are prepared.

7. **Attention getters**—There are many ways to get the attention of a group. You could make a sound or noise purposefully or by "accident." You could stand or sit, depending on what others are doing. You could do something unusual such as put a lampshade on your head or spill a drink on someone. You could have your cell phone ring, playing your favorite song as the ringer. Some of these attention getters might enhance your ability to get your voice heard and some may make it less likely anyone will take you seriously. You need

to make good decisions if utilizing attention getters to enhance your chances of being heard.

8. **Weighing in**—Sometimes the best way to get attention is by being silent. Others will notice your silence eventually and it may result in the group soliciting your input. This can be a natural and comfortable way to get the attention of the group. You now have the advantage of already having heard the opinions of the others in the conversation and have a better idea of what you want to say about the subject being discussed.

9. **Finishing other people's statements**—This can be tricky and needs to be done carefully. Finishing another person's sentences or statement may demonstrate your full understanding of what the other person is trying to communicate and gives you your entrée into the conversation. It may also demonstrate that you have completely missed the other person's point.

10. **Getting on the agenda**—If you are going to attend a meeting in which you want to ensure that you will get a chance to be heard, you can ask the meeting coordinator to be included on the formal agenda. This way you will be scheduled to talk and will probably be assigned a certain amount of time to cover your topic. If you do this, be sure to come prepared to make a clear and concise presentation appropriate for the meeting and do it within your assigned time allotted. If you do not, you might find it harder to get on the agenda next time.

Life Strategy Questions

- How much of what you typically worry about in life actually happens?

- How could reducing the amount of time you spend worrying and channeling this energy into something more positive help the quality of your life?

- Is what you want, get, expect, accept, and deserve all consistent with one another? Which of these factors is out of balance with the others? How could changing this have a positive impact on your life?

- Who is really in charge of your life? Is this who it should be?

- Do you cause self-fulfilling prophecies to come true in your life? What can you do to correct these self-fulfilling prophecies?

- Are you guilty of institutionalized thinking concerning your values and beliefs? What might some of these be?

- Who is the "voice of authority" for you? Do you trust this "voice"?

- How can you utilize the advice provided in this chapter to ensure that you get your voice heard?

Walking Isn't Everything

CHAPTER *4*

Communicating Successfully

Every attorney who has ever presented a case in court seems to know that you should never ask a question to which you do not already know the answer. An attorney does not want to be surprised by new evidence or information that might ruin his or her case. By knowing the answer in advance, the attorney can come prepared to ask each subsequent question in a manner that elicits the evidence that best supports his or her client's desired judgment or remedy from the court. The point is that we need to communicate with a purpose or even a strategy in mind. You should have a goal in every communication that you engage in with another person. You goal may be as simple as just to stay in touch and see how the other person is doing. This is a perfectly good objective. Or your goal might be to discuss something of great importance and consequence. In either case, you have a goal or objective in mind that you are expecting to achieve in your communication.

So much of our success in our lives is about being able to communicate effectively with others and with purpose. In most situations in life, you will not know the answers to everything that you would ask others in your personal interactions like the lawyer in court. Nevertheless, you should ask questions that show that you are interested in the other person and his or her life. People's favorite subject is typically themselves. If you want to develop a greater rapport with someone, ask him or her about his or her life rather than try to tell him or her about yours.

Becoming more effective in your communications can help you better achieve whatever goals you hope to reach in life. To become a better communicator, you may need to think about communications a bit differently than you do now. You should think about your communications with others as an opportunity to learn more about other people. Again, asking questions about them is obviously one way to learn more about people and their lives. But there is so much more that you can possibly learn about others because of your communications with them. Gaining a better understanding about how someone might react in a future situation can be very useful and helpful to you, particularly if you need that person to help you reach an important goal in your life.

People provide many clues about what they really mean in their communications with us. It is up to each of us as students of human behavior to observe and utilize this valuable information. This is information that is readily available to anyone who cares to pay attention and learn more about other people. We are constantly being provided this information in every contact we have with other people. The challenge is to learn to use this potentially valuable information to help you build better relationships with others.

Part of becoming a better communicator is a matter of paying attention to what others are communicating to you in a variety of ways. However, how you may normally think about communications with others may not always be the most reliable way to understand other people. In reality, communication occurs on a number of levels.

Three Levels of Communications

An important concept to understand about communications is that you should not limit yourself to one dimension of a person's communications. For example, the common misconception is that you only need to focus on what words someone speaks to understand what is being communicated. However, the actual words that a person says are only one clue concerning the actual message that may be being sent. If that is the only thing that you focus on, you may be missing the real meaning of what other people are trying to tell you and overlooking valuable information that will help you really understand their message.

Studies have shown that there are a number of dimensions of communications when people talk to one another. The first dimension is the actual words that are spoken. Words are what we normally focus on in our communications with others. After all, we spend a great deal of our time during our formal education learning about what words mean and how to use them correctly when speaking. People learn other languages to be able to understand and speak words with those from other countries. We spend much of our social lives learning to be able to say the right things at the right times to interact positively with other people. We are often judged on the quality of our speech and mastery of our language. You would think that words are the most important part of our communications. Surprisingly, this is not the case.

The actual words we speak have been shown to communicate only a small percentage of the actual message received in face-to-face interpersonal communications. Studies have shown this amount to be only about 7 percent of the total message received. As incredible as this seems, when you begin to analyze how you actually receive interpersonal messages, this fact begins to make sense. Another person's actual words only tell one dimension of the communication.

Words can be viewed as the "what" of communications. Think about how many times the words that someone said were misinterpreted. How many times have you gotten the wrong message because you only listened to the actual words being said by the other person? We have all experienced some miscommunications probably more often that we would like to admit. These miscommunications are the root cause of many interpersonal problems. The reason for these difficulties is that we often focus too much on *what* is being said by someone and not enough on *how* it is being said.

The *how* of face-to-face interpersonal communications consists of two additional dimensions that are very often ignored or overlooked. The first of these dimensions are the voice inflections that accompany the words that are spoken. Voice inflection consists of such things that are commonly referred to as the tone, pace, speed, emphasis, etc. It is the way someone says something. The very same word can take on a wide spectrum of meanings depending on voice inflections. This is true even with a little word. Think about how the two-letter word "oh," said in different ways can take on entirely different meanings to another person hearing it spoken. Try this experiment yourself. Say the word "oh" differently, giving it the following interpretation or meaning each time:

- *"Oh"*
- Surprise
- Shock
- Pleasure
- Questioning
- Doubt
- Detachment
- Resentment

Communicating Successfully

- Anticipation
- Meaning the letter in the alphabet between N and P
- Meaning zero or nothing

It has been shown that this dimension of voice inflections comprises approximately 38 percent of the message received. It is obvious that *what* we say is not nearly as important as *how* we say something. However, we do not typically focus on this dimension of communications as much as we should. Too often, we are much more concerned about *what* we are going to say rather than *how* we are going to deliver the message. However, paying closer attention to *how* people communicate can provide extremely valuable information about how they really feel and what their resulting behaviors might be in the future. For example, following up on the exercise you just completed with the word, "oh," what do you think might be the likely next behavior of someone who just responded to an offer made to him or her with the voice inflection of doubt? It would seem very likely that whatever the offer was that it would be rejected. Paying attention to different dimensions of communications can make many behavior predictions easy to call.

One other dimension of face-to-face communications is even more influential than the other two. This dimension involves the non-verbal behaviors of people when speaking. If you have been adding up the numbers of the first two dimensions, you have realized that there is still 55 percent interpersonal communications yet to be accounted. As incredible as it might seem, over half of most interpersonal communications that people transmit and receive are based on non-verbal behaviors. People are usually even more unaware of the subtle but very meaningful messages that they are sending when speaking. Think about a time when you have heard someone say something but you were not convinced that he or she really meant it or was being sincere or honest. This occurred because you were receiving a "mixed message." The person's words were not consistent with his or her voice inflections and even more importantly with the non-verbal or body language messages being sent.

We do not have to take a course in body language to be able to interpret these messages, although this could be very useful. We are all communications experts to a great degree by virtue of being able to communicate with one another. We have been studying communications from the time we were born. We can tell the difference in someone's body language being defensive as opposed to receptive to others. We are observant enough to be able to tell the difference between someone whose body language is telling us that he or she agrees with us and someone who does not agree with us. For example, if we are talking with someone and he or she has his or her arms folded or legs crossed in a manner that appears to be creating a barrier between the two of us, this is a sign that this other person may not be agreeing with us. Conversely, if the person is leaning towards us and has his or arms unfolded and hands in an upward or outward position, the person is likely giving us signals that he or she agrees with us.

Facial expressions are another form of body language that are also an excellent telltale clue as to what a person may be feeling and perhaps not consciously expressing. Again, people are typically far more focused on their word choices and not really consciously thinking about these much more important dimensions of communications. If someone is making eye contact with us and smiling, it is more likely that he or she is open and accepting of our communications. On the other hand, if a person seems to be avoiding eye contact and he or she is frowning, this would be a good indication that there is not agreement.

If non-verbal communications determine such a large percentage of our communications, then what happens when there is no visual contact during communications such as when talking on the telephone? The answer is that most of the affect of non-verbal communications is transferred to voice inflections. The most important point to remember is that the actual words are not always the most important part of communications despite what our instincts might indicate.

This is why there can be so many communications challenges when communicating to other people via e-mail today. E-mail does not take into account these critical elements of non-verbal communications. If the information being sent electronically is just data that needs to be shared with another person, there is not a problem. There are no non-verbal messages that are being missed by using this form of communications. However, e-mail and text messages today are often used as a form of *written conversation*. People try to use e-mail or text messages as if they were talking over the telephone. Be careful, if you find yourself engaging in important interpersonal communications via e-mail or text messaging, as you may not completely understand the true meaning of what is being said without the benefit of these non-verbal messages.

Much *free* information is available to us if we just pay attention and utilize this valuable data to help us better understand others. We do not always have to be passive observers of other people's behavior. We can interact directly with those whom we wish to understand better. Even in the course of normal daily conversation, we can learn a great deal about a person. We can also ask questions or seek information that can help us become better communicators. We are simply showing an interest in that individual and trying to gain a better understanding of his or her behaviors to improve our relationship.

A communications model can help us be more effective in achieving these objectives. The following model will help you become a better communicator and reduce misunderstandings that can so easily arise in daily conversation. So many interpersonal problems are a direct result of miscommunications. By learning to understand the messages we receive from others, we can reduce many of the communications and interpersonal problems we face each day. The model is very simple but it does require some extra effort on each person's part to communicate more clearly and effectively.

There are two prime factors in any interpersonal communication—a *sender* and a *receiver*. In most cases, the parties will exchange roles of sender and receiver throughout the communication. Unfortunately, sometimes a sender will not relinquish his or her role to the other person. It is almost as if a filibuster is taking place on the Senate floor in Congress.

The sender is the person who is doing the talking at the time. The receiver is the listener. They are like a pitcher and a catcher in a baseball game. The sender delivers the communication and the receiver should be *catching* it. However, sometimes even in a baseball game, the catcher misses the ball. It might have been thrown poorly or the catcher just does not concentrate hard enough on the catching the ball. Our common sense would tell us that the sender is the one that has the harder task of the two roles. However, this is not true. Being the receiver or listener is actually the harder role. Listening is not a passive experience but rather requires concentration and action. This is why some people are not good listeners. They do not put forth either the commitment or effort to become a good listener. Listening also requires a more directive approach than may normally be applied in most interpersonal situations. By studying the communications model, you can become both a better listener as well as a communicator.

The information you learn because of becoming a more effective communicator can be invaluable in understanding other people. You might be surprised at how much of the communications directed towards you, you might be missing. In the following model, you can see the interchange and roles that both the sender and receiver play when communications takes place:

Step 1—Send Message

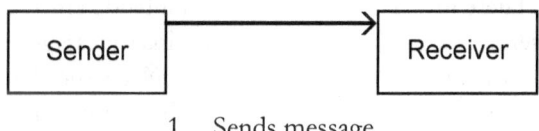

1. Sends message

Typically, this is where most people think that communication ends. However, effective communications does not end with a message being sent. Even more critical is the next step in the communications process:

Step 2—Receive Message

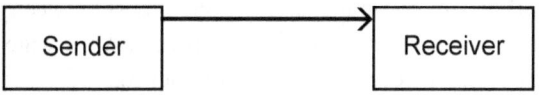

1. Sends message
2. Message received and interpreted

The intended receiver must not only receive the message but also understand its meaning. This is the greater challenge of the two steps presented so far. So many obstacles can prevent both the receipt of the message and its true meaning from being successfully transmitted from the sender to the receiver. For example, the receiver could be distracted and not even hear the message. There is often great competition for people's attention as they are bombarded with messages of all different sorts in their busy lives today. The other perhaps even greater challenge is that the receiver may perceptually change the intended meaning of the message. This relates to the previous discussion concerning the levels of interpersonal communications that takes place.

There may have even been an unintended message sent by the sender. This may be an unconscious message that the sender has conveyed concerning a particular issue that is the subject of the message. For example, the sender might have some very strong feelings about the topic that the message concerns. These feelings may be unconsciously transmitted in the message to the receiver. The receiver notices these feelings and perhaps gets a very different message than was intended. Understanding that this phenomenon does occur can enable us to become aware of the other person's true feelings about the subject being communicated to us without him or her being keenly aware that this has just been transmitted to us. As you can see, we can be better observers of other people's behaviors just by understanding and utilizing this communications model.

Typically, communications even at best between people usually end at this second step in the process. A message is sent and, hopefully, it is received. People do not usually feel that there is anything else they need to do to make the communications process work more effectively. However, at least two more steps are critical to effective communications occurring.

Step 3—Clarification

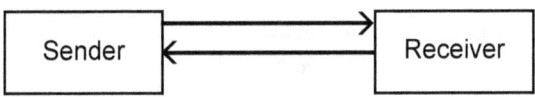

1. Sends message
2. Message received and interpreted
3. Receiver clarifies message

Effective communications begin when the person receiving the message requests clarification. In this step of the model, what is recommended is that the receiver actually asks the sender if what he or she heard was the intended message. This step in the process may go something like this, "I just want to make sure that I understand what you are telling me. I heard you say that …" This is an important step in the process because it is the only way that the receiver can be sure that what he or she heard was actually the intended message.

Step 4—Confirmation

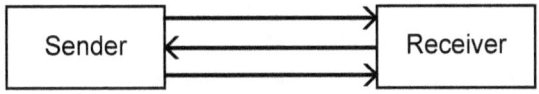

1. Sends message
2. Message received and interpreted
3. Receiver clarifies message
4. Sender confirms message

Winning Either Way

The last step in this communications process is confirmation. In this step, the sender confirms what the receiver stated was his or her understanding of the message. That is, assuming that the receiver heard the intended message correctly or at least to the sender's agreement and satisfaction. If not, then the communication process needs to begin again. This is the only way that there can be any degree of assurance that the message between a sender and a receiver is sent and interpreted correctly. The lack of these last two steps in the process is the cause for most if not all communications problems that exist between people. When you consider the different levels of communications described earlier in this chapter, it is no wonder that there are so many misinterpretations and misunderstandings between people.

> *There was a supervisor named Leon who worked in a small textile manufacturing facility in North Carolina who had a habit of asking his employees to repeat his instructions back to him after he was done giving them. Leon understood this last step in this communication model very well although he probably never saw it as diagrammed above. He just learned these principles from his years of being a supervisor and his frustration with people misunderstanding his instructions. By asking his employees to repeat his instructions back, Leon helped his employees clarify their understanding of his communications. His employees quickly learned to pay full attention to what he said for they knew that he expected them to be able to repeat them verbatim back to him. Leon not only taught his employees to become better listeners but he also helped them to become better able to perform their jobs because they clearly understood what was expected of them. There was far less misunderstanding or miscommunications on Leon's crew than in any other area of the factory.*

Communicating Successfully

Success in life is often a matter of communications. One of the ways to become a better communicator and ultimately to be able to get more of what we want out of life is asking the right questions. The most successful people spend as much or more time asking questions than they do giving answers. However, it is not enough just to ask the right questions; we also have to listen to the answers as well. So often, when we engage in communications with someone else, we are more focused on what we want to say next, than what the other person has to say. Effective communicators ask questions such as "Why do you feel that way" or say, "Tell me more about that." They listen unselfishly to what the other person really has to say. Less effective communicators are more focused on their own words and thoughts and say things such as, "You're not listening to me." What kinds of things do you find yourself saying during conversations with others?

We often may find ourselves involved in two different conversations—the one we are having with ourselves and the one we are supposedly having with the other person. We are too focused on what we want to say next and we miss what the other person is trying to communicate. We think too much about Step 2 in the model and not enough about Step 1. We walk away thinking, "Boy, that person didn't listen to a thing I said!" And likely, the other person left feeling the same way. If we want truly to improve our communications, we need to listen to what others have to say—even if we think we already know the answers.

Life Strategy Questions

- What behaviors do you display that project messages about yourself?

- Are you aware of your non-verbal communications?

- How do you approach interactions with others—are you open and approachable or more standoffish?

- Do you communicate better face-to-face, in writing, or over the telephone?

- Are you a good listener or do you want to do all the talking?

- To help determine this, do you find yourself saying things such as, "Help me understand why you feel that way?" or "Listen to me." The more you say, "Help me understand," the better listener you are.

- Do you use the word "you" more often than "I"?

- Do you avoid taking a contradictory or polarizing position before you truly know all the facts or reasons why someone else has expressed an opinion?

- Do you really listen to what other people are saying or are you thinking about what you want to say next?

CHAPTER 5

Strategic Relationships

Our relationships with others play a major role in the success and happiness we achieve in life. Many relationship problems are because people often act in unexpected and inconsistent ways. This causes many surprises and disappointments for those who are unprepared for such behaviors. Learning to expect the unexpected concerning the behavior of others can be an important skill for anyone to acquire. Learning to predict other people's behavior better can help us to understand them better, as well as deal more effectively in our personal interactions with others. Having a better idea of what to expect from others can also help us find ways to build stronger relationships.

Anticipating and even learning to predict people's behaviors can better prepare us for these challenging interpersonal situations. We have the advantage of being able to think ahead and plan our reactions rather than instinctively responding to others' behaviors in less than positive ways.

Winning Either Way

The following brief example illustrates just how frustrating it can be when people act in ways that are not anticipated or expected:

> *Karen Olson was a victim of the consequences of the behaviors of other people. She was constantly trying to cope with the unexpected behaviors of the people in her life. She felt as if she had little or no control over the actions of others. For example, Karen had a boss who was constantly surprising her with his reactions to certain events that occurred at work. She never really knew what to expect from him. It seemed that one day he would want one thing and the next day he would want something else. This was driving Karen crazy. In this regard, it seemed that Karen's personal life was not much better. Her family often made demands of her that she just could not seem to understand. It seemed to her that her spouse and children's needs were constantly changing as she tried desperately to balance the demands of both work and home. No sooner would she try to address their current needs than they would have new demands she never anticipated. This whole situation was a constant source of frustration and stress in her life.*

Karen's situation is not unique. Many of us try desperately to meet the expectations of others in our lives only to feel that we are trying to hit a moving target. What worked well yesterday may seem completely inappropriate today. People constantly seem to be changing their expectations and demands on a daily basis, if not even more frequently. How can we better cope with this dilemma? Anticipating the demands and needs of other people is one way to be better prepared to meet their expectations. In many ways, acquiring this skill is a selfish endeavor, and that is perfectly acceptable. Learning to predict other people's behavior creates a win/win situation. You can better meet the expectations of others while at the same time reducing the amount of stress and frustration in your life. This is a good thing, indeed.

Relationships

Our happiness and even success in life is built on our relationships with other people. Improving these relationships even to the slightest degree can have a significant impact on our happiness and sense of success. There is nothing unethical or manipulative in learning to predict the behaviors of others better. Rather, learning this skill can improve these relationships and reduce potential conflict and stress between us. Our interpersonal interactions will go smoother with less chance of misunderstanding.

Others will not necessarily be keenly aware of our newly acquired skill but likely will sense an improvement in our relationship. They may even take the credit for our improved relationship. If this is the case, we should let them have this credit. They played an important role in the process by the predictability of their behaviors. We may even be able to have anticipated that this would be their reaction. If this should be the case, we should think about how much better we would be able to deal with this reaction if we anticipated it rather than being surprised or caught off-guard by this response. This is the benefit of learning to predict others' behaviors. We can prepare and have a chance to respond in the most appropriate manner rather than instinctively reacting in a non-productive way.

Relationships are largely all about expectations. It is when expectations are not met that interpersonal problems exist. However, if our expectations are consistent with the behaviors of others, many of these problems may be averted. We will be less disappointed in others because we already anticipated their behaviors and will be better prepared to respond accordingly. Changing our expectations of others based on their behaviors can give us a great advantage when endeavoring to improve our interpersonal relationships.

Surprises

Surprises are fun when something pleasant and desired is presented unexpectedly to us. Birthday parties, a gift, a message from a loved one or friend, or a promotion are just a few of the best things in life that can come our way in the form of a surprise. However, surprises are not fun when they come in the form of disappointments in other peoples' behaviors. Being surprised in these cases causes us to be unprepared and to respond in ways that we may not be so pleased with afterwards. Surprise behaviors can be the demise of many relationships. Learning to predict other people's behaviors will help us avoid these unpleasant surprises and allow us to plan a more appropriate and productive response for the situation thoughtfully. Predicting other people's behavior is really all about expecting the unexpected. People may not always behave in predictable ways. However, understanding this fact can be an important first step in improving our relationships with others. If we can begin to understand in which situations someone may act unpredictably, we actually have significantly increased our understanding of his or her behavior patterns. If we expect the unexpected regarding other people, we may never be completely surprised or unprepared by their behavior.

Who has the ability to predict behavior?

We do not have to be clairvoyant to predict other people's behaviors. Actually, we already utilize this skill, probably on a daily basis. We are constantly making subtle, or not so subtle, predictions every moment we interact with others. This chapter will help you become more aware of the innate skills you already possess and allow you to develop them into conscious tools that can have a decided impact on the quality of your relationships

Strategic Relationships

with others. Behavior prediction skills are readily available and can be acquired easily. What is perhaps most important is a desire to learn to predict other people's behavior and understanding how this skill can be utilized to improve your interpersonal relationships.

> *A vice-president of a large corporation had a well-deserved reputation for being a very difficult boss. The human resources manager had his hands full trying to deal with all the problems this VP caused in the workplace due to his demands and temper. Members of the VP's staff often came to the HR manager to complain about their boss's typical abusive behavior and treatment of his direct reports as well as others. The HR manager would find himself commiserating with them, sharing his own emotional wounds received as the result of one of the VP's most recent tirades. However, after a while, he began to see a pattern in this executive's behavior. He began making mental notes on this pattern and realized that his behavior, although very disturbing, was also be very predictable. The HRmanager shared his observations with his coworkers who agreed with his conclusions about his predictability. They shared these predictable behavior patterns of the VP and even began challenging each as to who could predict most accurately the VP's response in a variety of future situations. By learning to anticipate these behaviors, they could develop their responses in advance to deal more effectively with the VP errant behaviors. Everyone seemed to get along much better as a result. The VP even seemed to have fewer temper tantrums.*

To Predict or not to Predict

The question is, "Should we attempt to predict other people's behaviors or not?" Only you can answer this question for yourself. However, here are several points to consider in pondering this decision. Why should we not utilize all of our abilities and intuitions about other people to improve our relationships with others? If this ability or skill will indeed help improve our relationship with someone else, would he or she not also benefit in the process? Finally, we are constantly predicting other people's behavior to some degree already, so why not learn to do it better.

The good news about predicting other people's behaviors is that often it really is not that hard to do with some thought and understanding. We do not have to have a degree in psychology in order to be a good student of human behavior. We just have to pay attention to a number of things that become readily apparent once we are looking for these predictors. In this chapter, a number of concepts are presented that can help you become more attuned to these behavioral predictor indicators. People do usually act in predictable ways. It is really just a matter of observing and noting these behaviors for future reference.

The concept of predicting others' behaviors is based on patterns. We are all programmed in some way to act in certain situations. This is based on a number of factors, including our past, successes, failures, expectations, goals, resources, etc. The following will help you be better able to factor in these variables as well as patterns in order to understand better how others may behave in the future.

In reality, we are all constant observers of human behavior. We study this subject every time we have contact with another person. Over the course of our lifetimes, we receive tremendous amounts of data on this subject. Although there are definite commonalities, each person we meet presents unique challenges to truly understanding human behavior.

Behavioral Patterns

People typically react in predictable ways. Again, stress can be a good example of one of these cues that begins a set of behaviors that if you take note will appear when these situations occur. You simply need to learn to watch for these behavioral patterns to emerge. This is where the cyclical nature of behaviors begins to become important to predicting other people's behaviors.

Sometimes it is very easy to predict people's behaviors when you simply think about how they have reacted to similar environmental cues in the past. For example, think about a sports coach who has a reputation for getting irate at the officials who regulate play in the game. Say that there is a controversial call made in an important game that potentially could cost the team a win. And just to make this example more interesting, say that this big game has championship implications. How do you think this coach will react in this situation? This would be an easy call indeed. You probably can also picture the coach's predictable apology to the players and others such as the media about his or her behavior and statements about how it was not really the appropriate way to respond in such a situation. Should you have any expectation that this coach will react any differently the next time he or she is faced with a similar situation?

And so it goes, behavioral patterns are established and repeated over and over. Why does this happen? Again, looking at the coach's behavior, perhaps this individual is programmed to behave in this way in such a situation. If all the elements exist to create such a situation, this individual will most likely, consistently, behave in the same way. Even if he or she tries hard to change his or her reaction to this type of situation, the tendency to behave in such a way will still continue and eventually become dominant. The coach may be able to control his or her emotions to a bad officiating call for a short period but eventually these irate behaviors will again emerge. This is not to say that people cannot or do not change—just that their natural tendencies to behave in certain ways can be very powerful and hard to alter. Observing and remembering people's behavioral patterns can give you great insight into how they might behave in the future. They may not even be as aware of their own behavioral patterns as you become.

Positive Relationships

Winning in life is really about having positive relationships with others. Thinking in terms of winning in your relationships with others should not turn into a win/lose scenario. Too often, social interactions are based on one person trying to find a win somehow over the over. This may manifest itself in competitive behaviors. This mindset is what more often than not destroys relationships. This pattern may be very hard to break. You might be able to establish or maintain a relationship based on this mindset but it will be problematic for at least one of you—probably the person on the losing end.

You can think strategically about your relationships the same as any other factor in your life. In fact, you can greatly enhance your relationships by thinking about them in this way. Every interaction you have with others should have a purpose to that relationship just like communicating with others with purpose. It is helpful to think of your relationships in a matrix view. The following Relationship Matrix can help you better understand how you can have more influence concerning your interactions and relationships with others.

The matrix breaks down our relationships as either casual or personal. Casual relationships would include those with whom we interact at work, acquaintances, friends of friends, etc. Our personal relationships would most definitely include our immediate and extended family members with whom we are close, friends, trusted confidants, etc. Along the continuum between casual and personal relationships can be combinations or variances of each type. For instance, we might have a close

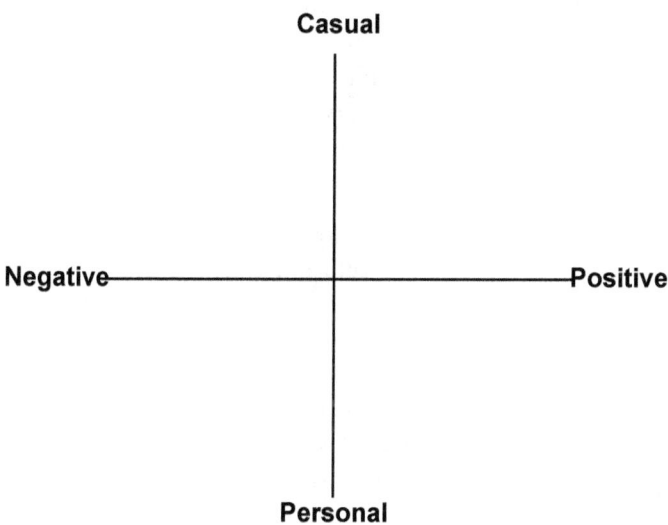

relationship with a colleague at work but not be friends outside the workplace.

On the horizontal axis is the differential between interactions with others in terms of positive and negative. Every interaction we have with others is to some degree either positive or negative. Obviously, our goal should be to have many positive interactions with others, both personally and casually. Unfortunately, this cannot always be the case. It may even be good to have some negative interactions with others, especially when warranted or necessary. To do otherwise might mean that we avoid conflict even when it may be a reasonable strategy considering the circumstance. Addressing a child's inappropriate behavior or standing up for oneself if confronted unjustly are examples of potentially appropriate negative interactions. Some amount of conflict in our lives is not necessarily bad. Conflict is inevitable in situations when people work and live together. Conflict can help get feelings out on the table or achieve better and more creative solutions to problems. However, conflict must not get to the point where it damages relationships. Learning to deal with conflict constructively and positively is an important goal in any interaction with others. Try keeping tack of the number of positive versus negative interactions you have for say a week or so. Then ask yourself if you are happy or satisfied with this balance?

The conflict matrix below shows six different approaches to dealing with conflict. In actuality, all of these approaches can be utilized to deal with and even resolve conflict. The application of each of these approaches to conflict may be determined by the situation or context of the conflict situation. Others of these conflict strategies are more appropriate in most potentially confrontational situations. Certain of these approaches are more productive and less damaging to your relationships.

Conflict Resolution Strategy Matrix

+			
	Reject	**Captions**	**Cooperate**
A S S E R T	**Oppose**	**Challenge**	**Compromise**
	Withdraw	**Concede**	**Disagree**
−		INTERACT	+

Strategic Relationships

Look at the vertical axis of this model labeled ASSERT. This indicates the degree, or lack thereof, of assertiveness one applies in a conflict situation to bring some kind of resolution to the issue. The horizontal axis on the bottom is labeled INTERACT. This indicates the level of involvement of effort the individual puts into bringing the conflict to closure. Each of the six approaches or strategies to conflict reflects varying degrees of both these ASSERT and INTERACT factors. For example, *Withdraw* is low in both ASSERT and INTERACT. In other words, it is the most passive and least involved of all of these approaches. Conversely, *Cooperate* is highest in these two factors, and in most circumstances, the best conflict resolution strategy to utilize.

An important point to understand about the matrix is that each of these strategies may be appropriate depending on the situation and circumstance. For instance, even the lowest levels of the ASSERT factor may be the best way to resolve a potential or actual conflict situation. Simply withdrawing or walking away may actually be a very good strategy if nothing positive is to be gained by being more assertive in our conflict resolution strategy. A situation in which someone is so upset that even trying to reason with that person would be an example when these strategies would be most appropriate. Looking at the lowest strategies in the INTERACT factor, to oppose or even reject may bring conflict to resolution by making clear your position on a particular issue even though this may not be a long-term solution. At least, everyone knows how you feel about the issue. In the middle of the matrix is *Challenge*. Challenge is a frequently utilized conflict strategy that shows disagreement but it does not necessarily involve solutions or problem solving. Becoming more involved as well as assertive in finding solutions through cooperation can lead us to more satisfying and permanent conflict resolutions.

Best Intentions

There are intentional and unintentional positive or negative interactions that people engage in on a regular basis. Sometimes, our best intentions do not always achieve the desired outcomes. We may unintentionally have a negative interaction with someone when our true intent was something very different. Others misunderstand us at times for any number of reasons. We can sometimes easily correct these misunderstandings by simply apologizing or explaining our true intentions. Understanding when we have created a negative interaction is important to dealing more effectively in our relationships. Too often, people are silent about their negative perceptions of their interactions with others. Understanding how others are reacting and perceiving us is very important to achieving better relationships.

Repairing damaged relationships is often a matter of clearing up misunderstandings or unintentional negative interactions. This is assuming that there is an interest in doing such a thing. It is acceptable to be satisfied with damaged relationships as long as there is no interest in improving the relationships. People sometimes agree not to like one another. This is fine as long as both parties feel this way—but what if you do not feel this way?

There needs to be a balance between negative interactions and positive interactions for a relationship to work. Obviously, the more positive interactions you have with someone, the potentially better your relationship. Consciously working on having more positive interactions with someone can help a previously damaged relationship as well as strengthen or nurture a currently healthy one.

People often have problems dealing with conflict with others without permanently damaging a relationship. It is possible to do this but the key is likely on what side of this relationship model most of our other interactions might fall. For example, if we typically find ourselves on the positive interaction side of the model, this relationship may be strong enough to withstand the negatives that a conflict situation might create. Dr. Stephen Covey, in his landmark book *7 Habits for Highly Effective People*, refers to this concept as an "emotional bank account." Dr. Covey likens this emotional account to a bank account in which we would invest our money. In this type of a bank account, we make deposits and withdrawals. We can continue to make withdrawals as long as we keep making enough deposits to keep from emptying out the account. Our relationships with others operate along this same principle. Thinking in terms of the Relationship Matrix, we need to make sure that our positive interactions stay ahead of any negative interactions we may have. The more positive interactions we have, the better able the relationship can withstand some conflict. Making positive investments in the relationship following conflict situations can also have a significantly positive impact.

Relationships are negotiable in that they can change at any time. We actually negotiate relationships in every interaction we have with others. We try to keep the balance of negative versus positive interactions in the plus column and minimize or rationalize the negative interactions. Disagreements between people are based on each person's perception of these interactions. People often try to rationalize or justify negative interactions based on the behaviors or actions of the other person. Avoiding the negative interaction in the first place would be far less complicated and supportive of the relationship. You will find that you are better able to have stronger relationships by thinking in these terms of positive and negative interactions and the balance you are maintaining between the two. Maintaining successful relationships is dependent on keeping this balance significantly on the positive side. You could actually set goals for yourself concerning this balance and work towards achieving them everyday.

Relationship Questionnaire

Referring back to the Relationship Matrix will help you better visualize where each of your relationships in your life may be placed on this model by thinking about how negative or positive your overall interactions and specific relationships might be in both your casual and personal relationships.

The following Relationship Questionnaire will also help you better understand your relationships with others:

1. Would you see a pattern or trend concerning your relationships if you plotted each of them on the Relationship Matrix?
2. What would that pattern be?
3. Would this pattern be different for your casual relationships from your personal relationships?
4. How satisfied are you with what this pattern might be?
5. Do you believe that there is a need to change this overall pattern in either your personal or casual relationships?
6. Has this pattern changed over time?
7. If this pattern has changed, what do you think has been responsible for this change in your relationship pattern?
8. How do you think this relationship pattern affects your life?
9. How could changing this pattern change your life?
10. How could you better achieve your goals by changing this pattern?

The results of the Relationship Questionnaire can be very important to you. You need to take a close look at your answers to ensure that you are doing what you really should or should not be doing to support these relationships in your life.

Strategic Relationships

Ultimately, your happiness will be dependent on your satisfaction with these relationships with others as well as with yourself. The real measure of success in life is in your relationships. If you win at the cost of your relationships, was it all worthwhile?

Balancing life's challenges

We all experience many different power struggles in our lives. We are pulled in many directions among our careers, our families, and personal needs or self. In the figure below, these aspects of our lives are shown.

However, what happens when these three aspects of our lives conflict with one another? When these struggles become overwhelming, people experience many different problems. In the next figure, we see a common situation where one's career overtakes his or her personal and family life. The

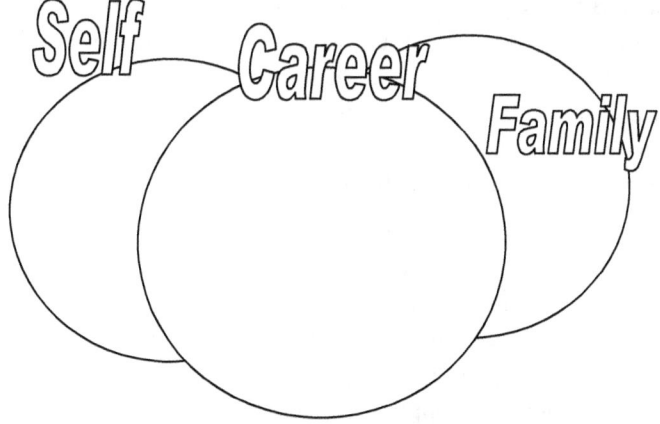

negative impact of this imbalance can present many problems. These can include stress, anxiety, and even physical symptoms and health issues. Balancing these potential conflicts is often the key to a more successful and satisfying life. Part of achieving this balance is accepting the fact that there will be times when things in our lives will become unbalanced. Life's necessities will cause this to happen from time to time. There are times when a problem or event in our personal lives will take center stage and demand all or most of our time. There are other times when the responsibilities of our jobs or careers may interfere with our personal lives and those of our families. On other occasions, we may have a personal need that needs to be addressed ahead of our other responsibilities. These things should be expected to occur in someone's life.

How prepared we are for these potentially conflicting power struggles in our lives will have a significant impact on our ability to deal with these potential conflicts. The key is balance. We need to maintain a reasonable balance between our careers, families, or personal responsibilities and selves. The more balanced our lives, the greater imbalance we are in a position to deal with, at least on an interim basis. If our lives are already grossly out of balance when a problem or challenge occurs in one of the other areas of our lives, the less able we will be to deal with this situation. For example, if our careers are already dominating our lives at the expense of our families and/or selves, a big problem at work demanding even more of our time will only continue to aggravate these other problems, perhaps even to crisis proportions. The result could be marital problems, behavior problems with children, health issues, etc.

On the other hand, if these other aspects of our lives are in balance, that is, we have spent time with our families and taken care of our health, we would be in a better position to be able to deal with the extra demands that our careers may be presently placing upon us at this time. Our families will be more understanding and supportive of our need to focus on our jobs now, even if it is at their expense. We may be physically better able to deal with the stress and demands that our jobs may be placing on us. In this scenario, it should also follow that when the problem or crisis at work is resolved that we return to a more balanced lifestyle in which we nurture all three aspects of our lives in reasonably balanced proportions.

Self-Relationship

Our relationship with ourselves is the most important relationship we will ever have in our lives. It also greatly determines how we come across to others and affects virtually every relationship we have with others. If one is not comfortable with his or her self-image, ultimately, self-relationship problems may manifest in any number of ways. Gaining a better understanding of ourselves is critically important to understanding others as well as our selves. Being comfortable with ourselves is perhaps the most important goal when it comes to succeeding in life. It is perhaps the greatest personal victory we can ever achieve.

A major part of taking control of our lives is accepting responsibility for what happens to us, both good and bad. This is the opposite of victim mentality. We need to take control and become accountable for our lives. If we depend on others to do this, we may become very disappointed. Think about how many people you know that wait for someone else to do something for them that will significantly change their lives. If this happens, then that is great. However, waiting or depending on others can be a disappointing experience. In actuality, the only person that you can truly depend on is yourself. You have the most stakes in the outcome of your life than anyone in this world. This is not to say that family and friends do not care deeply about you and your best interests because they may indeed. But the point is that you still need to accept the ultimate and, in some cases, the sole responsibility for your happiness and well-being. Others have

Winning Either Way

their own lives to worry about as well as yours. Every one of us needs to be self-centered in this regard.

What are the boundaries of this self-responsibility? Where does our sphere of influence concerning ourselves begin and end? Our lives and relationships are extraordinarily complex with interwoven interests and commonalities. This is made even more complex in terms of family dynamics. For example, the personal boundaries between parent and child can be as close to self-interests as humanly possible. For purposes of this discussion, the bonds between a parent and child are perhaps a unique exception to the boundary of self-responsibility.

That example not withstanding, we need to think about our own responsibility boundaries. Drawing these boundaries too narrowly or broadly can become problematic. For example, think of someone you know or have known that extended his or her boundaries too broadly. This person may have tried to be part of too many peoples' lives. He or she may have accepted some level of responsibility for so many people and things in life that it became overwhelming. This may have led to problems or disappointments on the part of those whose expectations of this person were greater than his or her ability to meet the expectations of others. Now consider someone you know or have known that had a much narrower responsibility boundary. This individual may have limited the number of people with whom he or she accepted any level of responsibility or relationship.

Our relationships with others bring with it certain responsibilities. Narrowing our relationship boundaries also reduces our responsibilities but also the rewards and benefits of these relationships. This is a balance in our lives that each of us must determine for ourselves. The most important thing is that we are satisfied with the relationship boundaries we have established or that have been established for us. If life's circumstances have somehow established these and we are not satisfied, then it must be up to us to change this situation.

Self-Images

Understanding another person is a complicated and complex challenge. People share certain things with others depending on their relationship. Understanding self-images can help us better understand not only others but ourselves as well. A person's self-image determines largely what kinds of messages he or she communicates to others. We will focus on three types of self-images: *Public-Self; Private-Self and Hidden-Self or Blind Spots.*

Public-Self

Public-Self could be referred to as the PR (public relations) types of communications that people exhibit. These are typically an extension of learned behaviors and are consistent with a persona or public image that a person is trying to project. One's Public-Self tells how the person wants others to perceive him or her. A person's Public-Self is on the surface and is readily accessible. Public-Self communications are sometimes practiced, even scripted, at times. These communications are often used and can be very repetitive. They are often the headline news of the day about an individual. For example, if someone were just married, this would be public information readily shared with just about anyone with whom he or she may have contact.

Similarly, news such as a promotion, transfer, new house, and even the death of a loved one are all examples of Public-Self information. Although, it may seem on the surface that we do not learn very much valuable information about someone by this level of communication, it can be extremely important in connection with other things we may learn or hear later. Public-Self information about a person could be considered to be above the surface communications from an individual. These communications are considered *above the surface* because they are as feelings said to be worn on a person's sleeve. It is like free information about a person, not hidden or private. These communications are there for everyone to see and hear. Public

Communications can help us better understand the *beneath the surface* communications that are part of the Private-Self aspects of the individual.

Beneath the surface communications, as the name implies, are not readily apparent. These are much more subtle communications that are not readily accessible to everyone. However, both above the surface and *beneath* the surface communications are important to understanding others as well as ourselves. We need to be conscious of our public selves and conscious of how we come across to others. Our public selves are the part of us that most people get to know. How we perceive our public selves ourselves is important to many or most people. Sometimes, we spend a great deal of time, effort, and even money trying to create a certain public image we wish to project to others.

Private-Self

Private- Self involves aspects of us that are much more personal and not as readily shared with others. However, some people are more prone to sharing this information with others. We have all encountered that person who, within minutes of meeting us, tells us his or her entire life story. Most people are not quite so open about sharing these personal details of their lives. Private-Self Communications are typically *beneath the surface* communications. Often, it takes a certain amount of time, even years for someone to trust another person enough to share these intimate details of his or her life. Sometimes you really cannot truly understand another person without at least some understanding of this information. This information often gives us that glimpse into the reasons why a person behaves the way he or she does. It may help you better understand why unpredictable behaviors from this individual occur.

Hidden-Self or Blind Spots

Hidden-Self, as the name implies, is all about information about the individual that is not necessarily above the surface or below the surface. Then where is this information about the person and how is this information communicated? These are often buried communications. This information may not even be readily apparent to the individual. Curiously, this may be information that is often known to others but not to the individual. These are what are often referred to as *blind spots*. Everyone may realize or know something about the individual but that person. Perhaps he or she refuses to acknowledge this information or does have some understanding but will not accept the truth.

People often attempt to present public facades about themselves that nobody buys. It is like the balding man who parts his hair above his ear and sweeps it across his head in a futile effort to hide the bare spots on his head. Everyone knows that the guy is bald and he is not fooling anyone with his attempt to hide this fact, but he does it anyway for reasons of his own.

Hidden Communications may not always make sense or seem logical to others. They do not have to. They serve a purpose for the individual and that is all that is important. Nevertheless, these hidden communications can tell us a great deal about the individual just by the fact that he or she has elected to pursue these behaviors. For example, the person who refuses to accept the reality of his or her physical aging process may be reluctant to accept other realities that relate to similar aspects of his or her life.

Self-Perception Model

In the model below, a person's Public-Self, Private-Self, and Hidden-Self or Blind Spots are illustrated. As shown on this model, Blind Spots can occur in both the Private-Self and Public-Self. There can even be Blind Spots that encompass both the individual's Public-Self and Private-Self. Regardless, they can still be just as obvious to everyone but the individual.

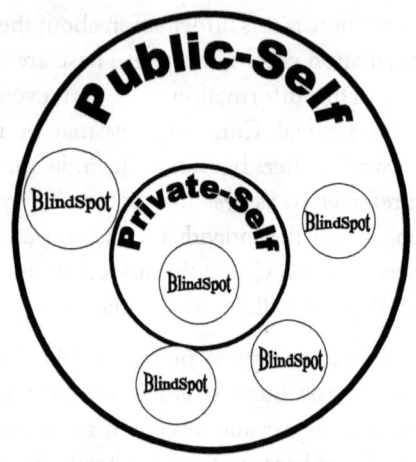

These self-images are important to understand for a variety of reasons. They help us better understand a person's behaviors. This information also helps us understand what is most important to an individual and even what he or she may be refusing to accept or admit about himself or herself. This can be a valuable glimpse into the personal values of the individual that is available to you by simply studying his or her behavior and making a few simple observations. The better you understand someone's behavior, the more likely you will be able to really understand him or her and build a better relationship with that person. Understanding these things about ourselves is also invaluable.

The following is a story about someone with a blind spot that everyone else seemed to see except him. What do you think would eventually happen to this person if this blind spot continued to dominate his life?

Strategic Relationships

Chris Johnson was a well-liked person both in his professional and personal life. He had a beautiful family and good career. He was also very ambitious. He worked hard to be successful in business, climbing the corporate ladder faster than most of his peers. Immediately upon meeting Chris, you would get the impression that this was a young man with great aspirations and a promising future. He stood out among the crowd as somebody going places.

However, there was another side of Chris that you would not see on the surface because of how hard he tried to make a great impression on others. He was actually very insecure about his success. He was constantly worrying about how fast he was advancing in the company and how successful he was, compared to his older brothers, best friends from college, and even neighbors. Chris was the type of person who worried about being shown up by a neighbor's new deck or expensive sports car in the driveway. He was constantly searching the latest and greatest new status symbol to impress others.

People sometimes would comment on Chris's ultra competitive nature. Even his boss would worry that he was at times too aggressive in business dealings even though this typically was a desired characteristic in his sales role. The boss just wished he would tone it down a bit. Chris's wife felt the same way. She was more than satisfied with their lifestyle and wished that Chris would just be more satisfied with what they had rather than constantly pushing for something more. His huge ambition and competitiveness were getting to the point that it was beginning to affect his relationships with others.

Home life was becoming more stressful all the time. His expectations of his family were as great as or even greater than they were for him. His wife worried about the effect that this was having on their children. Even his golfing friends were beginning to wish they had never invited Chris to join them for their regular

> *Saturday round of golf. Although they all enjoyed a little competitiveness among the four of them as they played, Chris took this to a level that was no longer enjoyable. It was hard to have fun being around Chris if he was not winning all the time.*
>
> *The funny thing was that Chris did not seem to be unaware that his behaviors were becoming a problem for others. He would just assume that others were jealous or envious of his accomplishments. He ignored their subtle comments or messages concerning his behavior or dismissed them altogether. In fact, Chris was personally very pleased with where he was in life at the time and did not think he had any problems that he could not handle himself.*

There is no question that our relationships are the most important aspect of our lives. Thinking about relationships more strategically can help us improve them and enhance our lives in many ways. Creating goals focused on these relationships can be extremely beneficial. Learning to understand others and their behaviors better can help us improve and nurture our relationships. In addition, improving our relationships with ourselves will help us in our relationships with others in our lives.

Life Strategy Questions

- Do you believe that your relationships play a major role in the happiness you achieve in life?
- How can better understanding others help you build stronger relationships with others?
- Are you satisfied with the balance of positive and negative interactions you have with others?

Strategic Relationships

- How could clearing up misunderstandings you may have with others help repair damaged relationships?
- What information do you publicly present to the world and is this consistent with your private-self?
- Are you comfortable with your self-image?
- How is your self-image different from your public-self?
- What are your blind spots?
- Do your blind spots interfere with your life?

Winning Either Way

CHAPTER 6

Finding Your Life Strategy

Finding our strategy in life is like trying to find our groove. In many ways, it is something that really cannot be expressed in words. Our life strategy is a dynamic and complex concept, yet it can be simple at the same time. We already have a strategy whether we are aware of it or not. It is what we think about when we make any kind of plans or decisions. We do things that are consistent with our life strategy and avoid that which is not. You may be wondering, "How could I have something so important in my life and not be aware of it?"

Even if we are not keenly aware of having one, when we really stop and think about it, we do have a plan in life. Perhaps you are a student studying for a future career. Or maybe you are just starting out on your own in life or beginning a family. Perhaps you already have children you are raising or approaching the end of your career and thinking about retirement. Whatever the case, you have some kind of picture in your mind about what you would like the future to bring for you and your loved ones. You may not think of it in these terms but this is your life strategy. Most people do not think about these thoughts as being strategic and perhaps they are not. Becoming strategic in your life strategy thinking can make a significant difference in achieving your goals in life.

Strategic thinking is about thinking ahead. It is about putting things and time into perspective. In other words, thinking in terms of how things you do today will influence things that will happen tomorrow. The problem that most of us have is that we do not look that far beyond the immediate. We are too focused on today's issues and do not give enough thought about how we might be affecting our future. This narrower mindset is the basis for the problems that many people experience in their lives.

Time

Thinking strategically means that we are factoring time into our present decisions and actions. We have to respect time. Time is the most powerful change force in the universe. Everything changes with time. Time is all a matter of perspective. We need to think about how things will be not only today but also in the future. Time, despite all of the science fiction books and movies that fantasize the contrary, is unpredictable. Thinking strategically involves considering how things may look to us in the future. No one can tell us with certainty how things will turn out in the future but giving things enough thought could help us make reasonable assumptions. Another important factor to consider is that our perspectives about things will change over time as well. We may not know exactly how we might feel about something in the future but like predicting people's behaviors, we can make some reasonable assumptions.

Think about the game of soccer. The basic object of the game is to move the ball towards the goal. The ball is the center of attention. Everyone wants to get to the ball. If we watch inexperienced players, we will probably see everyone rushing to where the ball is at any given point in time during

Finding Your Life Strategy

play. But is that really the best strategy for being successful as a soccer player? No. The better strategy would not be rushing to where the ball currently is but to where it is going to be. We will find that more experienced players are very adept at anticipating where the ball will be and getting themselves there. We need to be constantly going to the ball wherever it may be.

Too many people spend their lives going to where the ball is now rather than where it is going to be in the future. They always seem to find themselves a step behind everyone else. They are too present-day focused and not strategic in their thinking. They think in terms of how things are, not what they are going to be. The following brief story illustrates such an attitude:

> *Mary was always thinking about today. As a young adult, she pursued with passion whatever she wanted as if there was no tomorrow. Her finances were a disaster. She was constantly maxing out her credit cards or emptying her bank account. If she saw something she wanted, she bought it. Mary gave little or no thought to whether she needed or really wanted something, she just followed her instincts. She would take risks that most people would not. She was constantly living in the moment.*
>
> *Those who knew Mary worried about her impulsive behaviors. But others admired her free spirit and willingness to take chances and enjoy life without worrying about the consequences. Her parents were concerned that Mary was not thinking enough about her future. "What will ever become of Mary if she doesn't change?" they worried many times when hearing about their daughter's latest antic or dilemma in which she found herself as a result of her attitude about life.*

Four Success Factors

Successful people generally have a plan, in fact, a strategic plan for their lives. They understand that success is often a state of mind, a vision, an attitude that enables them to be successful. They also realize that success is also matter of the following four factors of *timing, circumstance, opportunity,* and even *luck*.

- **Timing**—Timing they say is not everything—it is the only thing. Timing is very important in any plan. Studying the lives of highly successful people will reveal that timing played a big part in their success. If the timing had been different, they may not have been able to amass their great fortunes, reach positions of power, or become as famous. Having a sense for what time would be the best to pursue a goal or even dream is very important to achieving desired outcomes. Although we may not be able to control the timing of most events, we can control our decisions and actions in relation to the timing of certain events or occurrences. Successful people see opportunities where others do not. They recognize that the time might be just right for something to happen. They capitalize on this timing and succeed as a result.

- **Circumstance**—Just as with timing, we may not be able to control all the factors that exist in any situation but we need to be able to recognize when certain circumstances exist. Identifying what circumstances need to exist for success can be critically important in making decisions that can affect our future. Making decisions or initiating a plan in the wrong circumstance can have disastrous results. If the right circumstances do not exist, we may be destined for failure before we even begin. Circumstance in this sense is often the catalyst that makes something else work. All of the other elements must be present, but if the right circumstances do not exist, then it may all be for naught.

- **Opportunity**—There is another old saying that opportunity knocks but once. If opportunity does happen to knock on our door, we need to get up off the couch and answer it. If not, then we need to go out the door and seek it. Successful people do one or the other. Too many people spend their lives lamenting about the opportunity that got away. Their attitude is that this opportunity lost is lost forever. They spend the rest of their lives on the couch never hearing the doorbell ring, much less answering the door. In reality, opportunity constantly knocks but we have to be able to recognize it when it does. Opportunity may come disguised as other things, often as a problem. Successful people see opportunities that others miss or fail to act upon when opportunity knocks.

- **Luck**—You cannot dismiss luck as a big factor in being successful. In just about every successful person's life story is an element of luck that played a significant factor. But why is it that some people seem to have all the luck in life? Is it possible that to a certain degree we make our own luck? It is like the golfer who said, the more I practice this sport the luckier my shots seem to become. Bad luck, if there is such a thing, cannot become a deterrent to success. Bad luck may just be the fact that the other three factors of timing, circumstance, and opportunity just were not yet present or not in the right combination. The stars, so to speak, must all be aligned in certain ways that enable success to occur for someone but you also must put yourself in the position to be lucky.

You have to be willing to pay the price of success, whatever that might be. Too often people impose self-restrictions upon themselves that become the most limiting factors in their lives. They accept defeat before they even begin to plan strategically to reach their goals and objectives in life. They chalk it up as bad luck about which they cannot do anything.

What proportion do you think needs to be present of each of these four success factors in order to achieve your goals for success? Is it possible that any one of these factors alone could enable success to occur? Of course, this could happen. Think about someone winning the big jackpot in the lottery. Winning the lottery is just a matter of luck. In this case, being lucky can reward you with millions of dollars. However, the most likely answer to this question is that all four Success Factors normally need to be present in relatively equal proportion to enable success to occur. This is why success is not something that happens easily or for everyone, even if they are deserving of success. Despite your best efforts, one or more of these factors may not be present or at least in great enough proportion to the others to enable success to occur for you. Someone could have the best idea, service, or product available but if the timing is not right, no one may be interested in buying. The circumstances that might currently exist may make whatever you have to offer the world less desirable. There just might not be any opportunities available regardless of one's credentials or qualifications. And sometimes just plain bad luck (which might be the absence of any or all of the other three Success Factors) may prevent success.

Success Strategies

Understanding that there are factors that need to exist for success to happen, you still need to do certain things to optimize your chances of achieving your goals in life. The following are four strategies that can lead to success in life:

Finding Your Life Strategy

Study > Service > Retire

Most people pursue this strategy for success in their lives. It has the highest probability of success of all four of the strategies. It is based on the *Earn* side of the Life Strategies Model introduced in Chapter 2. This strategy says that you need to prepare for life by getting a good education or training, work hard to excel at your job or vocation, and get to the point when you can retire and enjoy the fruits of your labor in your later life. Luck does play a factor in this strategy but success is much less dependent on this factor. Putting yourself in the right circumstance at the right time is important to the success of this strategy but you have to be prepared for the opportunities that might come your way.

Entrepreneur > Develop > Profit

This strategy is on the *Negotiate* side of the Life Strategies Model. The classic example of this strategy at work would be the person who goes into business for his or herself. This would include anyone who is not on someone else's payroll. Doctors, lawyers, dentists, storeowners, company owners, or anyone self-employed would fall into this category. The goal or even dream of many people is to move from the Study>Service>Retire strategy to this one.

Invest > Risk > Interest

This strategy is less focused on working for a living and more on getting what we want on a faster schedule although it could be combined with the previous two life strategies. Some may work for a living and at the same time have an investment strategy as well. This can be a good combination of strategies providing for ways to achieve both what we need in life as well as what we want (see Life Strategies Model). There can be any number of ways that one can pursue this strategy, such as investing in stocks and bonds, business ventures, real estate, art, precious metals, etc. However, each has some level of inherent risk. We could be putting at risk that which we worked so hard to earn by pursuing the previous strategies but there is also potential interest or payoff. Typically, we hear more often about the person who reached the big payoff than about those who lost their investment.

Talent > Fame > Fortune

This strategy is not for everyone but only those who truly have a special or uncommon talent. The problem is that there are many hopefuls or wannabes who think they have the talent to pursue this strategy. It is understandable why someone would want to pursue this life strategy for it has the potential for huge payoffs including fame, fortune, and the adoration of others. Actors, actresses, models, athletes, perhaps even some politicians would be included as pursuing this life strategy. Obviously, not everyone who pursues this strategy is going to be successful—only the truly talented or very lucky.

Inherit > Win > Find

This is the easy way to be successful, at least financially in life. However, as the lives of many of those who have been afforded this luxury in life have shown, it does not necessarily lead to a happy or fulfilled life. Perhaps it is the absence of having to achieve one or more of the other strategies that causes this to occur sometimes. There may be a lesson here that things coming too easily in life may ultimately not be the best way to find happiness despite how attractive this strategy may look to others.

Whatever our strategy might be, we need to keep a number of things in mind to help make our plan come to fruition.

Finding Your Life Strategy

Facing Your Fears

Many people do not try to reach their goals because they are afraid of failing. In their minds, failing would be the worst thing that could happen to them. But in reality, failing is not the worst thing that could happen. The worst thing that could happen is not even trying to reach realistic life goals. We do have to go for broke in a high stakes poker game; we just need to pursue our dreams.

This can involve any number of things, such as planning to open our own business with the proper planning and resources, getting additional education or certification, improving our health by exercising, building closer relationships with family and friends, or countless other things that we can do to enhance our lives. But we need to put our chips on the table, so to speak. In other words, we need to try at least to make our dreams become a reality. We need to do things to make them happen. We need to tell the world, or at least those in our lives who would be interested, what plans and goals we are pursuing and ask for their help and support. This is the first step towards reaching our life goals and often the most difficult.

Control Your Destiny

The very first thing that we need to do is to understand that we and we alone control our destiny. Sure, any number of factors and circumstances, some of which were previously mentioned in this chapter, come into play. But the point is that there are variables in every situation or circumstance that can be controlled or at least managed. Identifying these variables is often the key to success. Once identified, we need to act decisively.

For example, say that someone believes that he or she is in a career believed to be going nowhere. This person may worry that he or she will be stuck in this dead end career. This person's boss does not appreciate or support his or her efforts despite considerable effort expended on the job. The employee keeps asking for additional training believed essential to performing the job successfully. This individual feels underpaid and unappreciated. It is futile to ask for a raise after having been turned down in this request so many times in the past.

Now let's take a closer look at this situation and analyze it a bit more carefully in terms of what is controllable and what is not. We could break down this problem into the following components:

- Boss
- Training
- Pay
- Growth
- Work effort
- Personal Satisfaction

Can we control the boss? Probably not directly, but we could try to change his or her opinion or feelings about our potential and contributions on the job. How could we do this? There are many books and courses available about impressing our boss, but perhaps the best way to do this is to listen to what he or she expects of us. Ask the boss for clarification concerning these expectations. If the boss really thinks we are interested in meeting his or her expectations, this will likely increase the chance of additional support or even training that could help us in this regard. The boss may not be supporting additional training because he or she is not convinced it would result in what he or she expects or wants accomplished in your job. This could lead to the boss finally paying attention to your efforts and hard work. The boss may feel that you are now *getting it* concerning his or her expectations. This could lead to more recognition and a better chance for pay increases in the future, all of which leads to greater job satisfaction and growth.

The point is that just putting more effort into something often is not the answer. There is a key to just about any problem or situation that we need to find that could improve or even correct a problem we may be experiencing. The trick is finding this key. The key in this story was a lack of understanding about exactly what it was that the boss really wanted. Too often, due to a lack of communications, people appear to be seeking the same goals but have entirely different perspectives on the matter. In this case, the boss must have had different expectations about the job.

When Our Best Efforts Fail

Why is it that so often our best efforts seem to fail when we try so hard to be successful? Is it that we may be doing the wrong things? Does everyone else seem to know something that we do not? Are we the only ones who do not seem to have a clue as to what we should do? The answer to all of these questions may be "yes."

All of us have certain *blind spots* about ourselves that we are not keenly aware exist. This is another example of everybody, but us, seemingly knowing something about us. In reality, you probably are somewhat aware of your blind spots. You probably know all too well what your weaknesses and strengths are. What you probably do not do is to think about these very often. You are most likely more focused on other factors that perhaps are less likely to yield the desired results you are seeking. You may drift to your comfort zones of behaviors or tasks that you enjoy the most or come most naturally to you. This is a good thing most of the time. You want to focus on your strengths not your weaknesses. This helps you find a positive rhythm in your life. Establishing a rhythm in your life is important. We find comfort in rhythms. These rhythms create natural routines that we learn to depend on in our lives. But when these rhythms are interrupted, this can throw you for a loop.

We often experience stress with these cyclical rhythms in our lives. Think about how difficult it is to break a habit. A habit is a rhythm of sorts. We perform habits on a routine basis often without much thought to these behaviors. They become part of our lifestyle. Often we are less willing to negotiate away these life rhythms, whatever form they may be in our lives. These rhythms sometimes prevent people from trying something new. People may deny themselves opportunities because they do not want to interrupt these rhythms in their lives.

In their new book, *Now Discover Your Strengths,* Marcus Buckingham and Donald O. Clifton explain that it is not particularly productive to focus too much on trying to be good at something that does not come particularly naturally to us and not pay enough attention to what does come naturally. It only makes sense that if we put all our energies into improving things we do not do well presently, that at best, even if successful, we may only learn to do these things in a mediocre manner. Is that really our goal—mediocrity? On the other hand, if we focus on developing our strengths, the things we already naturally do well, we have a greater chance of really excelling in these areas. These may become the differential between us and everyone else.

But our blind spots are important to understand and accept. They may be the things that might be limiting our success or reaching goals we hope to achieve. This is not to say that we must master our blind spots, but we do need to address their existence. We may need to compensate for them by some other skill that we possess. Or we may need to neutralize them to the point that they no longer are a limiting factor. If we do not and just continue to ignore blind spots, we may find ourselves in a state of denial and this is not a good place to be. Learn to understand and accept your blind spots. Work on them to

Finding Your Life Strategy

the extent that you need to but do not try to do something or become something that you can never really accomplish.

The real key is finding something that everybody does not already know or is not presently doing but that is needed. This is the key to the success of authors, musicians, comedians, business opportunities, and scientific discoveries. The best negotiators find the key that others are seeking or even have not discovered yet. The problem is that it seems like every time we hear about a good idea, somebody else has already thought of it!

In order to avoid this, we have to do our own research. We do not have to come up with a revolutionary idea that changes everyone's life or habits but we do need to think ahead. This is all part of becoming strategic in our lives. Again, we do not have to have a crystal ball to give some good thought to what might likely happen in our lives.

The older and more experienced we become, the wiser we also grow. There are obvious, or at least readily apparent, patterns that emerge. As discussed previously, even people act in quite predictable manners. All of life is a big cycle. We need to step back and see these cycles emerging in the people and world in which we live. Taking all of these things into account, we should be better able to read the tea leaves, so to speak. In other words, when certain things line up in certain ways, we need to be able see that a pattern is emerging.

The world can be predictable to a certain extent when we look at things in this manner. We might even send up trial balloons just to test out our theories or predictions. This could be done in any number of ways including asking questions to confirm our assumptions or suspicions about what is about to happen. For instance, if you believe that you have identified a pattern of behavior emerging, test it out. Ask the person what he or she is planning to do next. You may know before they do what their next behaviors are going to be!

Winning Either Way

This type of knowledge or sense can be extremely helpful in reaching our goals in life. Better understanding not only others, but also ourselves, can be a huge advantage. How we utilize this knowledge can be a determining factor. It might be a matter of our negotiating DNA. Our negotiating DNA is our propensity to try constantly to get a bigger better deal out of just about any situation. We need to know when to try to get something better and when to be satisfied with what we have. It is like playing poker in the high stakes game of life. We need to make sure that we are not going after things that do not really matter—distinctions without differences. What this means is that if you are going to pursue something with earnest, make sure that it is worth the effort. You do not want to end up winning the battle only to lose the war or fight battles over things of little value or importance to you.

For instance, too often, we get committed to things that just do not have any real meaning in our lives. We take positions and fight battles that have little or no real importance in our lives. Conversely, we may become too passive about other things of genuine meaning in our lives. Understanding this distinction is tremendously difficult but crucial. This is where simple strategic thinking can again be very important and beneficial. If we just take the time and effort to think things through and what the likely outcomes might be, we can make much better decisions in this regard. We will find it amazing just how easy and enlightening this simple exercise can be.

So often, we find ourselves in arguments of convenience. We fall into a syndrome where we find ourselves taking a position on something just because we think or believe we are supposed to think this way. Maybe this is programmed or habitual thinking or we are voicing a position that we heard someone else that we admired take in the past. But we need to stop and question if we really feel this way. We need to be careful what we ask for because we might just get it! You need to make sure that you are negotiating for what you really want in life not just what someone thinks you should want.

All of this can have associated risks. Really being honest with ourselves about what we want in life may both surprise ourselves as well as others. We are potentially exposing the *real* us. Life is all about making the right choices. Of course, we will not always make the best ones, but we need to learn from each choice we make. Just as being thrown off the horse, we have to get right back on. But before we do, we should think about why we ended up on the ground and what we are going to do to prevent the same thing from happening all over again. This is perhaps the point that many people fail to realize. We cannot keep doing the same things that resulted in less than favorable results in the past and expect the outcome to be different in the future. We have to change our behaviors if we ever expect to change what we get in life. This is hard to be sure, but also very satisfying and beneficial.

Taking control involves making these kinds of changes. We can turn defeat into victory by changing our attitude. This may mean that we need to change our attitude about ourselves. We need to think of ourselves as winners. We need to approach situations with a positive, winning attitude. Anything less is like conceding defeat before we even begin trying. Setbacks should be thought of as nothing more than learning experiences that will help us achieve our goals next time. We should not settle for anything less than what we expect ultimately out of life.

However, we need to keep sight of our priorities. Too often, we are so wrapped up in the process that we lose sight of what we were trying to achieve in the first place. Often, we have already reached our priorities in life without realizing it. People become overachievers striving for greater and greater goals than they ever really intended to reach in the first place. Sometimes, reaching too grand of goals can become self-defeating. Getting our lives out of balance for too long is not really reaching our goals if it costs us things that are of great value to us. Be careful about striving to reach your goals. Make sure that you keep your true priorities in mind.

Not meeting your goals may not always be the worst thing that can happen to us. Losing may be the best thing that could ever happen. Think about the simple twists of fate that brought you to where you are right now in your life. Think about how just a minor change may have put you in an entirely different place right now. Simple twists of fate can be fateful. Moving with, rather than resisting, these twists and turns in life can help the process go more smoothly and more enjoyably. Letting our lives take us where it is naturally going with a little guidance from us may be the best strategy we can ever create.

Life Strategy Questions

- How have the Success Factors in life of timing, circumstance, opportunity, and luck affected your life so far?

- How could you change the influence of one or more of these factors on your future success?

- Do you believe that you control your destiny? Why or why not?

- How could not meeting your goals turn out to be a good rather than bad thing in your life? What are some examples in your past?

CHAPTER 7

Negotiating Life Strategies

We not only need to have a strategic plan in life but also one that is negotiable in the sense that it needs to be adaptable. We do not always get what we want in life but we can have more control over things and events than we may presently believe. This is true regardless of our circumstances. You can always do something to impact the situation.

> There is a story of two prisoners in a dungeon whose hands were chained and hanging with their backs against the wall. They were starving and barely clinging to life. One says to the other, "Hey, I've got a plan." Now that is strategic planning!

Negotiating life strategies is personal, private, and fungible, meaning replaceable and changeable. Most people think of negotiations as a win/lose situation because of our competitive nature. A better model is what *should* happen in a real estate sale in which both parties get what they want. Typically, the seller sells his/her house at a fair market price and the buyer gets a new home believed to be worth the cost. Both parties leave satisfied. Problems are only created when one or both of the parties in the deal becomes unhappy or dissatisfied. This might happen because one or the other of the parties begins to believe or realize that the price was not fair. The property may not live up to the advertised claims or the property may become worth much more than the buyer paid.

This is a good analogy for describing a successful life strategy. A person seeks something in life and by virtue of earning or negotiating achieves his or her overall life's objective. This is a balanced life equation. This equation does not balance when people do not get what they want or expect. The problem with the equation may be either perceptual or real. Perceptual problems are created when someone becomes dissatisfied because his or her expectations may have changed.

Reaching your goals can be a disappointing experience if you have unrealistic expectations concerning what life may be like when they are achieved. People sometimes fall into the "if only I could _____," everything would be great then. The blank could be filled in with any number of answers such as make a fortune, win the lottery, find a better job, or meet the right person. Goals are not necessarily the key to happiness. Happiness is a state of mind that we must create for ourselves. External influences will probably not make us happy.

Happiness comes from within. Negotiating life strategies is all about finding this happiness despite the external forces and factors in our lives. This is not to say that we should necessarily be satisfied with just any result or circumstance. We have the right to seek and ultimately get what we want. The point is that we should not make the goal everything in our lives. Our happiness should not be contingent on reaching some level of success or goal. We determine our happiness independent of these factors. If we reach our goals, then all the better. This is the best life strategy we could ever find. Any discussion about

Negotiating Life Strategies

negotiating life strategies must keep this important concept in mind. It will make being successful in negotiating our life strategies much more likely and achievable.

Reality Checks

Sometimes, we need to take a moment for a reality check in our lives. A reality check is when we look to see if what we are striving to achieve or expect is realistic. This is not to say that we should be less ambitious or give up our dreams but we also need to be realistic about these things. For example, if we do not have the physical ability to be a professional athlete then pursuing such a goal would only result in frustration and certain failure to reach this goal. In addition, by focusing our time on this unrealistic goal, we might be denying ourselves the chance to reach a more achievable goal. In the end, we lose both ways.

We should be looking at reality checks from time to time just to make sure that our goals are reasonably achievable. The problem with reality checks is that often other people are trying to provide them to us without valid reasons. They obviously do not understand our determination, potential, and rationale for pursuing our dreams and goals. Reality checks must come from within with a full understanding of these personal factors. Only we can decide if a goal is realistic or not. We should listen to the advice and input from others but not allow others to make such important decisions for us. Once again, this is analogous with the "when to hold 'em and when to fold 'em" philosophy of playing poker. We need to know when we have a winning, or potentially winning, hand and when we should be looking for new cards to play.

Ten Reality Check Questions Every Person Should Ask When Pursuing a Goal

1. *Do I have even the remotest chance of reaching this goal?* Despite all the motivational lectures or slogans you may hear, certain things just are not obtainable. Pursuing the impossible will most likely result in failure or even worse may cause other problems in your life. You may put too much on the line trying to achieve an unrealistic goal or objective at the expense of more realistic ones. You might be ignoring other important things that need your attention and time that will suffer for no gain in the end.

2. *Is reaching this goal going to be everything I expect it to be?* You need to be prepared for *post-goal letdown*. Like many things in life, the pursuit, not the obtainment, of things is often the most exciting. People often are not as happy or satisfied with what they obtain as they thought they might be beforehand. Reaching one goal usually sets the stage for the pursuit of another goal and so the cycle continues.

3. *Is there any downside to reaching this goal or objective?* You need to think about potential downsides to reaching the goal that you may not have anticipated. Are there things that you might not like once the goal is reached?

4. *What might be the unanticipated consequences that might occur?* As they say, every action has a reaction. Reaching a goal may cause something you have not yet thought of to happen as a result. This unanticipated consequence may be something that you may not really want to have happen. What might these things be?

5. *Am I prepared for the changes that may come as a result?* Most people, if they admit it or not, really do not like change. Change causes us to leave what we are comfortable with

Negotiating Life Strategies

and venture into the unknown. Think about what changes this goal might bring into your life.

6. *Do I really know what I am getting myself into?* Have you really checked into what will be involved in this goal? Do you really understand what may be expected of you or how it will affect your life and relationships?

7. *Am I truly committed to this objective or direction I am taking?* Just how committed are you to this objective or goal? Are you willing to pay whatever price it will take to get there? When things get difficult along the way to achieving this goal, will you still feel that it is all worthwhile?

8. *How will important others in my life react or respond?* Ok, say that you have become comfortable and fully committed to this goal or objective. What about those important others in your life? How will your family and friends be impacted? What sacrifices will they have to make? How do they feel about it?

9. *Am I prepared not to achieve this goal?* How mentally and emotionally invested are you in the achievement of this goal? If you do not reach this goal, how will you handle it? Will you let this disappointment negatively affect your life or will you accept it and move forward towards other objectives?

10. *Is this really my goal or someone else's?* Are you pursuing the goal because you want to or because someone else important to you wants you to? It is perfectly fine to pursue what someone else wants you to do as long as you feel that the goal is just as important as the other person does. You need to own your goals. You are the one that will have to deal with the consequences of achieving or not achieving the goal, whatever they might be.

Bigger Better Deal

Many people spend their entire lives trying to find that bigger better deal. They are never satisfied with what they have regardless of what they may have already accomplished. They kid themselves that finding this bigger better deal may bring greater happiness or contentment. In reality, reaching that bigger better deal may only raise the expectations bar for that individual. They may consider merely reaching previous lesser goals once thought to be accomplishments now become failures. This mindset can only result in a sense of failure sometime in this person's life journey.

There is bound to become a point when reaching that next level of accomplishment may not be possible or even realistic. In business, this is called the *Peter Principle*. Employees continue to be promoted until they reach their level of incompetence. In other words, once they finally reach a level in the organization at which they are no longer able to perform competently, they stop getting promotions. Our past successes sometimes deceive us about what realistically to expect ahead. We set unrealistic goals that set us up for almost certain disappointment. Instead of setting such lofty goals, we would be better served setting more realistic and obtainable goals consistent with our accomplishments. Taking that occasional time out for a reality check might make our pursuit of goals more satisfying and rewarding. Dream big, but do not make your happiness or feelings of self-worth contingent on reaching unrealistic goals or accomplishments.

> *Ted Edwards was always an achiever. He was a high school football star, honor student, one of the most popular kids in his class, and president of his senior class. It was no surprise that he was accepted into a top university and graduated at the top of his business class. The major corporations who came to campus and had a number of attractive job offers recruited him before he even*

graduated. He accepted the best paying job and relocated to the corporation's headquarters in a large eastern city. He earned his MBA in the evenings and began to rise rapidly in the company. He married his college sweetheart and they began raising a family. Life, it seemed, was good for Ted and his family.

But there was another side to this story. Ted had an insatiable desire to succeed. One success only led to the pursuit of another. He became a perfectionist in every aspect of his life. Even his wife and children had to try to meet his demanding standards of behavior and achievement. He felt that this was the least that they could do considering all the advantages and benefits in life his success was providing for them. He was even more unrelenting with his subordinates at work. His constant demand for higher standards both earned him a reputation for getting things done right and for being an unreasonable boss. However, his considerable talent combined with his huge ambition soon got the attention of the top executives of the company. Soon Ted was named vice-president of one of the major operating divisions in the company. It was not too many years before he left the organization to accept the chief executive officer position with another company. Obviously, with all this success came considerable financial benefits as well.

The only problem was that neither he nor his family was happy. He and his wife seemed to grow farther and farther apart the more successful he became in business. Perhaps he was just too involved in his work and not enough in his family anymore. His job demanded considerable time away from home and family. He justified this as the price they had to pay for the financial advantages his job provided. But if you asked his wife and kids, they would have said they would have traded these things for a happier home life, one without the stress and conflict that existed in theirs. After a few years, Ted's wife asked him for a divorce. He lost his family in large measure due to his great success in business. He wondered if it was all worthwhile and if he would do things the same way if he had the chance.

The Romantic Comedy Dilemma Decision

Nearly every romantic comedy movie seems to have this basic plot—the main character is faced with the life dilemma of giving into the pressures of family and friends and settling for someone who happens to be available at the time or waiting for Mr./Ms. Perfect to come along. Of course, in the movies, just when it appears he/she will never find true love, along comes Mr./Ms. Perfect and they live happily ever after. Unfortunately, real life is not always like the movies. We have to make many decisions that seem like this same dilemma. Do we take the sure bet or wait for something better to come along? This dilemma is not simply limited to finding our life's mate but many other less important decisions as well. Jobs, purchases, moves, investments, etc. all can present this same dilemma. How we react in these situations may be determined by our risk tolerance (as well as how many romantic comedy movies we watch!).

To help you deal more decisively, you need to consider the following questions before making such important decisions:

- What I really want?
- What I really need?
- What I would agree to?
- What I might end up with?
- What I think I can get?
- What I don't want to lose?
- What I am willing to put at risk?
- What I have to gain?

Negotiating Life Strategies

Based on your answers to these questions, where would you place your current thinking concerning the decision on the following continuum (you can be at any point along this continuum)?

Reject------------------Consider------------------------Agree

Negotiation Determiners

A number of determiners influence our risk tolerance concerning our propensity to negotiate for what we really want in life.

- **Values**—In this sense, value means how important something is to us. The greater we may value something, the less likely we might be to negotiate it away.

- **Expectations**—Often, we get what we expect in life. Our expectations can cause us to reach our goals in that they cause us to behave differently. Expectations can make us more determined to get the things we want and value the most.

- **Beliefs**—Our beliefs can be the strongest forces in our lives. If we believe strongly in something, we also may be far less likely to be willing to compromise.

- **Needs**—We need strong motivation for achieving goals. Needs are different from wants. Needs are typically not negotiable. We have to have what we need. People are usually willing to do whatever it takes to get what they need.

- **Goals**—Goals are often more negotiable as they change throughout our lives. Our goals need to be consistent with our values, expectations, beliefs, and needs. Understanding that some or even all of these above factors can change throughout our lives, so too will our goals.

Think Politically

Like them or not, you can learn a great deal from politicians. Politicians understand the importance of image. They understand that how voters perceive them will be the determining factor in whether they are elected or reelected to office. They understand that perception is reality to voters and work hard to build the right image that will attract voters. The successful ones learn to use sound bites and photo opportunities to their advantage to help create this desired image. Politicians also campaign for their agendas. Their agendas consist of what they supposedly stand for and support. They work to create or institute certain laws or legislation that they believe in or feel that their electorate believes in that will keep them in office. They also understand just how quickly and fickle public opinion can be at times.

How can political lessons help us manage our lives better? Thinking politically can be a very useful strategy for us to follow. Think about how you may already be utilizing many of the same strategies that politicians do in your life. In one fashion or another, you probably already campaign for the things you want. For example, if you have ever tried to make the case at work that you should get a promotion or raise, you undoubtedly spend time on a campaign trail of sorts trying to convince your boss that he or she should support you. You likely became more aware of the image that you were projecting to the decision makers in the organization. You may have pointed out to others the many contributions that you have made in the past as well as your potential in the position you seek. If you did this well, you paid attention to what was important to your boss and tried to support his or her agenda. You also were conscious that your boss had others whose wants and needs must be addressed and worked towards achieving this objective as well.

We also need to think politically in our personal lives as well. It might be a little much to expect our friends and family to wear campaign buttons supporting us but we do need to solicit their help and support. They need to understand what we believe in and even what we stand for. They may not always completely agree with us but at least they need to understand what we represent as people. Even more importantly, **we** need to understand what we represent as people.

We need to think about our agenda much the same as a politician does. Our agenda may be simple and there is certainly nothing wrong with that. For example, our agenda might be to support and take care of our families. Additionally, our agenda may be to aspire to a certain position or to achieve other personal goals. Whatever our agenda may be, we should pursue it with the same passion and enthusiasm that a politician would when seeking election.

However, unlike some politicians who fail to fulfill campaign promises, we need to honor the promises we make to others who support us. Nothing will cause us to lose the support of others faster than reneging on a commitment or promise. Even our image is important to others in our personal lives. Image in this sense goes beyond just wearing the latest fashion or style. This image is more about how others perceive us. Do they think of us as someone on whom they can depend or someone who will support them unconditionally? Or do they have some other image about us? It is important to think about what image we may project to others, especially those about whom we care. Ask yourself, "Am I satisfied with this image?" If the answer to this question is anything less than "yes," you need to think about how you can change this image to something that you are happy or at least comfortable with. It is truly unlikely that that there is anything more important for you to pursue in your life than reaching this objective.

1-800-SUCCESS

Wouldn't it be nice if life came with guarantees that we will be happy or we would get our money back like in one of those infomercials you see on television late at night? Happiness could be as easy as dialing 1-800-Get-Rich or 1-800-SUCCESS. Life is not an infomercial and being highly successful in life just is not that easy. However, despite how irritating these programs can be sometimes with their grandiose claims, there may be a few lessons you could learn from these infomercials:

Think Success

We watch the infomercials that are really neither a program nor a commercial, probably because we want to believe their claims. We want to believe their claims of extraordinary weight loss without dieting, creams that will make us look years or even decades younger, or overnight wealth with no money down. The point is that they give us positive messages that we can achieve our goals. They give hope for those who may have given up trying to achieve their dreams. Perhaps this is their greatest benefit to those who dial their toll-free numbers for a money-back guaranteed trial of these products. If these products actually deliver on their promises for the majority of customers may be another matter, but they do give people hope that will can improve their lives. Hopefully, consumers are not too disappointed in their results or do get their money back as guaranteed.

Do Something Different

Infomercials get people to do something different, to try something new. They tell people that there is a different and hopefully better way to reach their goals. They try to convince viewers that what they have to offer is better than what they tried in the past. The entire focus of an infomercial is to get people to pick up the phone and call to order the product. This, they say, is the first step to a better life. Again, this may or may not be true but these infomercials do get people to go into action.

Take the Initiative

Infomercials are designed to convince us that we need their product to improve our lives. They try to convince us that purchasing their product is the best thing we can do to achieve our goals. Infomercials tell us to take the initiative to improve our lives. If we do not do something, we will remain just as we are, which presumably is unhappy with our current lives, which for some reason, their product can improve. Infomercials are a call to action for the viewer sitting at home watching television to do something, get off the couch, pick up the telephone and begin a new life.

Market Yourself

The producers of infomercials are usually great marketers. They know exactly how to make the product appear attractive and appealing to viewers. They know just what "buttons" to push to try to entice viewers to call and purchase their product. They do this with creative approaches to selling. They know that they need to stand out among the countless other vendors selling very similar products, also with guaranteed claims for success. They set aggressive goals for success that attract customers. A viewer may not get very excited about losing five pounds of weight during the next several weeks but the thought of losing twenty or more pounds in such a short period may just be too much to resist. Finally, they present positive images of what their product has done for others. They present testimonials of customers who claim to be delighted with the result they achieved because of buying the product.

Much of being successful is convincing others (as well as ourselves) that we can be. Taking a few tips from the producers of these infomercials can help us be better marketers of ourselves.

What would happen if you produced an infomercial about yourself? What would it look and sound like? Think about the following questions about this infomercial about you.

- What claims would you make about yourself that would help market you to others whom you would like to impress?
- What would you advertise that you could do for others?
- How would you get the viewers' attention to pay attention to your infomercial?
- Whom would you pick as a celebrity endorsement?
- Who would give testimonials about you?

Do not Defeat Yourself

Too often people defeat themselves by having a *defeatist* attitude about their goals and aspirations. Infomercials address this problem in buyers' minds. They give viewers hope when they may have given up ever solving their problems in life. Changing our mindsets from a defeatist mentality to a positive or possibility mentality is the first step towards improving our lives. Perhaps these negative thoughts or attitudes have been with us for all or most of our lives. Maybe others put these ideas in our heads. It does not matter. We can change the way we feel not only about ourselves but also about how we interact with others. We can change the way we perceive the world and the possibilities it may hold in store for us. Once lost is not always lost. Just because we had a problem or an image of ourselves in the past does not necessarily mean that we must perpetuate it in the future.

On Hold

Often, things are put on *hold* for any number of reasons. These holds prevent progress toward whatever goal or success we may be seeking. Our goals get temporary delayed or ended altogether. These holds cause us to have to wait for something to happen. Moving forward towards our goals must involve resolving or eliminating these holds. For example, someone may not be able to complete a home remodeling project because a certain part that he or she needs may be out of stock at the local home building store and needs to be ordered. The entire remodeling project may have to be placed on hold until this part arrives and the sequence of work on the project can continue.

Think about how many things in your life are put on hold because of such a situation. We find that we are constantly waiting for something to happen in order to proceed with what we want to do or have happen in our lives. How much control do you have over these *holds* in your life? Think about how many of your goals are currently on hold for one reason or another. An example of such a hold might be not getting a college degree that would open up countless career opportunities or not learning a particular skill or technique that could be important to your advancement. On the other hand, it could be some self-improvement goal you may have set for yourself that would give you more confidence. The most important question is, "What can you do to eliminate or expedite these holds?" How much control or influence do you have over the factors that are creating these holds to exist in the first place? How many of these holds are caused by you? Are you delaying or avoiding doing certain things in your life that are limiting you? What can you do to eliminate these barriers, move forward, and continue towards reaching your goals?

Decisions

In many regards, our lives are the sum results of all of the decisions that we have made previously, both good and bad. If we look back at where each decision we have made has taken us, we would see a pattern in our lives. This pattern generally shows what kind of decisions we make in different situations. We may have made some decisions that we now see with the benefit of hindsight as being good decisions. We may also look back and see other decisions that resulted in less than positive results. We obviously cannot go back and change decisions we have already made but we can try to make better decisions in the future.

> *There used to be a television commercial for an insurance company that portrayed a young woman talking to her older self. Her older self was giving her advice on decisions she should make as she lived her life with the benefit of already knowing the outcomes. Obviously, one of the bits of advice was to purchase this company's life insurance at an early age. But to make the commercial more entertaining, the older self also gave her younger version advice on some other things including her love life and current boyfriend. By the way, the older self's advice was to dump the boyfriend!*
>
> *Think about if you could somehow have a conversation with your older self. What questions would you ask? What would you be most curious about finding out concerning important decisions you are making today? What do you think some of these answers might be? What would happen if you could talk to your younger self? What advice would you have given yourself looking back? How would have following this advice impacted or changed your life and where you are today?*

Negotiating Life Strategies

The most successful people have a *pattern of success* in their lives. Most likely, these patterns of success are based on making consistently good decisions that are aligned with their goals for success in their lives. They avoid making bad decisions that would be counterproductive to these same goals. They have a plan upon which every decision they make is based. They also usually have a backup plan just in case things do not always go as expected. They are able to make alternate decisions that do not take them off track from their goals. They do something about what they do not like about their lives and are not willing merely to accept defaults. Unfortunately, most people do not have a plan, much less a decision-making process to help them make the right decisions in their lives.

Having a Decision Process can help us make better choices in our lives. The following simple model can help you with your decisions in the future:

Decision Process

Options → Influencers → Alignment with Goals → Expected Outcomes

Understanding this Decision Process

Options

First, you should consider all of your options. Often, we make hasty decisions before such consideration. Deciding too fast or without contemplation likely is the cause of most poor or even bad decisions made in life. You probably have more time than you think to make even the pressured decisions you are faced with in life despite what others may tell you. Remember, pressuring someone to make a quick decision is a negotiations tool or ploy. Do not be fooled.

However, there are moments of opportunity that once gone may be gone forever. For example, you may have but a limited time to make decisions to accept a certain offer or make a purchase due to others considering the same option. Recognizing these situations is obviously important but you need to understand the difference between real decision urgency and being pressured into believing the decision is urgent. Ask those that portray urgency to explain what the basis of this urgency is and evaluate the legitimacy of their rationale.

Influencers

Typically, many other people influence our decisions. Usually, we get more advice than we need or want from others. This can be very frustrating, even annoying. We may value the advice of certain people more than that of other people. Sometimes, we may immediately tune out or dismiss a person's advice without really listening or giving it consideration. Conversely, we may listen and follow other people's advice simply based on trust or our relationship with that person. However, the best advice on advice is to listen to all of the advice that we might receive. Consider the advice based on the advice and not necessarily the source of the advice. The best advice we may get can be from unexpected sources.

Indirect influences may also be directly affecting us. The situation, or related situations, may also have an influence that we need to consider. Do not just look at a decision one-dimensionally or in the instant moment of the decision. Think about decisions in terms of the time and place in which they are made, remembering that these factors quickly change. Think about the decision in terms of how it impacts the future and where you might be. If you feel that the decision will still be a good one in terms of these factors, you can be more assured that you are making the best choice today.

Alignment with Goals

There should be a certain alignment of the decisions we make and our goals in life. We should ask ourselves if the decision is consistent or inconsistent with these goals. Will this decision move us closer to achieving our goals or farther away? Or is the decision contrary to these goals? Making a decision that is not in alignment with our goals may still be a good decision but we should think about what it might do in relation to our goals. For example, if our goal is to save enough money to make a major purchase in our lives and we decide to make a big purchase on something else, we need to think of the consequences to our original goal. If there are reasons for which we are comfortable with this decision, then this is fine. However, if we come to regret our decision or feel that we have compromised our original goal, then this decision may not have been such a wise decision. Considering these things as part of our decision-making process will help us avoid regretting decisions later on.

Expected Outcome

Just as dealing with people, predicting outcomes is not always as difficult as we might think it would be if we give something enough careful thought. Often, just talking something through and discussing the various alternatives will bring us to expected outcomes. Just thinking strategically about the potential outcomes is a worthwhile effort. Play things through in your mind. Think about how others might react. Think about other consequences or results of your decisions. Think about how it might impact other things or events. Think about what might be the unexpected consequences of this decision. Just considering these factors can give you good insight into the possible outcomes of a decision. Obviously, if your conclusion after considering these factors is that a decision may not be a good one, then you should reconsider the decision. Talking things through with another person can also help lead you to predicting expected outcomes with reasonable accuracy.

> *"If we do this, Jack will have a fit!"* Sarah said to her colleague Mark.
>
> *"Yea, I know. I don't want to be in the room when he is told that there is going to be a delay in the launch of that new product line. Let me know what happens,"* Mark replied.
>
> *"Oh, no, you don't! You're going in there with me. I'm not facing him alone when he hears the bad news,"* Sarah replied.
>
> *"You know something; maybe Jack won't be so upset after all,"* Mark wondered aloud.
>
> *"What do you mean? You know how upset he gets about setbacks like this,"* Sarah questioned.
>
> *"Well, I'm not sure that Jack is really convinced that we are ready for this product launch right now. I have heard him stressing over getting everything done on time to be able to meet all the deadlines we are facing. Not being completely ready may turn out to be a disaster of greater proportions than moving the product launch late,"* Mark concluded.
>
> *"You make a good point, Mark. Do you think that Jack is going to be all right with this news?"* Sarah asked.
>
> *"Let's go find out,"* Mark replied.

As this dialog between Mark and Sarah proves, talking something out often leads us to logical conclusions that we may never have reached otherwise. Sharing ideas and insights with others can help us collectively come to reasonable assumptions and predications about outcomes. What do you think Jack's likely response may have been to the news that the product launch had to be delayed? Perhaps even more important is how could Sarah and Mark's prediction about Jack's reaction help them when approaching him with the news? Do you think that if they approached Jack in a more positive manner when presenting this news to him that he might receive it better? How might have this different approach influenced Jack's reaction and subsequent behavior?

Despite the advantages we can gain by thinking strategically about outcomes, a certain degree of unpredictability will still exist. There will always be the unanticipated, the surprise, and the outcome nobody ever predicted or perhaps the silver lining that supposedly exists in every cloud. We always need to be prepared to be surprised. Sometimes these surprises might be pleasant and sometimes not so pleasant. Thinking through the possibilities of just about any situation can help us find good results even in unlikely circumstances. For example, when an economic recession or downturn exists, many potential financial problems for people are associated with this event. However, there may also be opportunities that the situation may create depending on our circumstances. For example, if we are looking to buy something of value, such as real estate, we might find that prices are favorable for us as buyers. Of course, the reverse will also be true for the seller. It just depends on where we are at the time. We may not be able to control the circumstances of every situation but few cannot be improved by trying to find something that may not always be obvious to improve the situation.

This is what can be called a *Life's Oxymoron*. Oxymorons are words that appear contradictory but they are used together anyway. A Life's Oxymoron is a situation in which certain things are happening but should not result in the way they do. This is similar to a team turning what appears to be certain defeat into victory, working against great adversity to prevail, or turning

Winning Either Way

one's life around in a positive manner. Sometimes, what appears to be the worst thing ends up being the best thing that could ever happen. Some things that happen in life defy prediction. The point is that we need to be trying constantly to find ways to improve or succeed regardless of how things may appear. So much of dealing with even the most challenging situations is our attitude and how we react to the situation. Believing that we can succeed is most of the battle.

Once again, the key is always to have a contingency or back-up plan. Just as the Boy Scouts' motto says, "Be prepared." This plan should be one that we would be happy, or at least content, with either way it turns out. The more we can have some control over the outcome, the more satisfied we will be with the result. The problem for many people is that they do not do enough or any contingency planning. They do not have a Plan B much less a Plan C or D. If we do not have a back-up plan for ourselves, then someone else may create one that may be far less acceptable for us.

As much as possible, we want to be on our own agenda not someone else's. The key is to create our own agenda. Again, being both pro-active and strategic in our lives is critically important. In the following brief story, this young man had a goal in life but also developed back-up plans that eventually came to reality. Without developing alternative strategies, he might have found himself discouraged about life at a relatively young age and might not have found a successful alternative to his plan for his life.

> *Kevin Johnson had planned on going to medical school ever since he was a little boy. He studied hard in school trying to get good grades particularly in biology and chemistry, and he did well. After graduating from high school, Kevin was accepted into the college of his choice that had a strong pre-med program. Kevin's college years went well, even though he found many of the classes*

> in the program very challenging. Nevertheless, Kevin worked hard and graduated with above average grades. However, getting into medical school was very competitive. The top students from universities all across the country and world vied for admission into the better medical schools. Kevin just could not compete despite all of his dreams and best efforts.
>
> Fortunately, Kevin had an excellent guidance counselor in college. She was aware of how competitive it was to get into medical school and had encouraged Kevin to have a back-up plan just in case the inevitable occurred. She guided him into a minor study in business. She encouraged Kevin to think about how he could combine his interest in medicine with an interest in business. She suggested a number of possible alternate fields such as pharmaceutical or medical equipment sales, research, teaching, or a number of other possibilities he could pursue just in case medical school did not come to fruition.
>
> Kevin had researched these possible fields and had a good idea of which ones he would pursue if he did not get into medical school. He eventually went to work for a medical equipment company where he became very successful and satisfied with his career.

Risk Tolerance

Just about everything discussed in this book is a matter of one's risk tolerance. Some people are willing to take greater risks than others are. They believe in the old adage, "no risk—no gain" and they may be right. On the other hand, there is a certain comfort knowing that we are going down a predictable path with very reasonable expectations for success. Which life philosophy we adopt and to what degree we are willing to take risks is a personalized matter. Only you can truly decide where you fall on the risk tolerance model shown below. However, your risk tolerance, as so many other concepts discussed in this book, is something about which you should have awareness. You need to be both conscious and comfortable with how you do or do not exercise your risk tolerance. You may discover that you presently have too high or too low of a risk tolerance and want to change your approach to taking risks.

As this model illustrates, the greater the risk, the greater the potential for rewards or loss. Is the greater potential to lose what you placing at risk worth the potential gains? Where would you place yourself on this chart regarding your risk tolerance concerning reaching your goals in life?

Up your Aspirations

Experienced negotiators are usually willing to accept some level of risk to reach their goals. When presented with a compromise, they figure they already have the deal being presented. Their goal is to improve the deal not just settle for the compromise. However, there may be nothing wrong with settling with compromise, depending on our goals and objectives, especially if we have a lower risk tolerance. Even getting to a compromise often requires a great deal of work. A compromise typically involves each side giving up something. Getting the other side to concede anything might be a monumental task. Not agreeing after trying so hard to get them to budge even a little bit might be a bad idea. It could cause the entire negotiations process to break down, ending in a stalemate.

Life is actually full of compromises. We do not always get exactly what we want in life. Most things are a trade-off of one kind or another—a compromise of some sort. When we go to a job, we give up our time and energy in return for the pay and benefits we receive. We give up our hard-earned money for the things we want to purchase to make our lives better. We do things for other people to support and nurture our relationships. All of this is part of the normal balance of life. We have to do certain things to get certain things from life. Interfering with this balance can cause things to get out of balance. Just try not reporting to work and see how this balance of job and pay becomes unbalanced in a hurry.

Now let's look at the other side of this life balance equation. What would happen if you looked at this balance differently? What would happen if you changed the balance to increase your aspirations? Instead of doing just simply what is necessary to keep this balance, what would happen if you did more than what is required? Would you tip this balance in your favor? Could you get more out of your job or career by doing more than just keeping things in balance? What about your relationships? Could you do more to nurture your relationships? What would be the result of improving these aspects of your life but putting more into your side of this balance equation?

Too often, we negotiate compromise out of our lives. We do the same things and expect different results. Think about what you really want in life and what it might take to get it. But you also need to keep in mind that your goals change. Priorities are often on a sliding scale. What once may have been a top priority for you may no longer be important at a different time in your life. You need to keep in touch with your priorities and goals to make sure that they are still what you really want. Not being aware of what is important to you presently can make achieving goals unfulfilling. Keep in touch with your goals and priorities on a constant basis. Do you really want the same things that you used to? Think about where you are going to be next and what you may want or seek at that point in your life. Visit your goals on a regular basis. Do not feel bad if they change. It

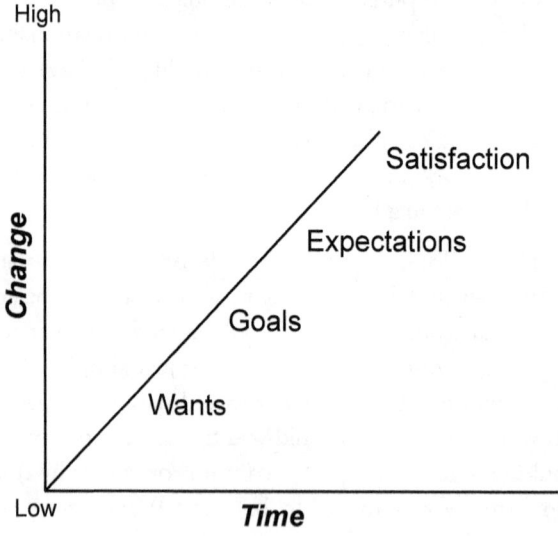

is ok if you do not want the same things that you used to want. Things change in life and so do you.

What this Priorities Model illustrates is that getting what you used to **want** may no longer be such a satisfying thing today. Our priorities change over time. Looking more closely at this model, you will see that at the most fundamental level, what you want changes over time. Just think about how important something may have been to you at one point earlier in your life that may have little or no meaning to you today. With these changes, your **goals** in life become modified. You no longer seek the same things that you may have at a different time in your life. Your **expectations** from life also are different at each point along this continuum. Finally, how **satisfied** you are is a function of your priorities. Whether you are achieving or reaching your priorities in life at a certain point in time may determine your level of satisfaction.

The problem is that sometimes we do not adjust to this sliding scale of priorities. People may not really be aware of the changes that occur during their lifetime. They seek the same or similar goals that they have had all their lives. This is not to say that we do not have core values that we learn from the time we are born and that guide us throughout our lives. These may never change. But there are things that we may want at a time in our life more than we want anything else that will have a very different value to us at some other point in time. Staying in touch with this sliding scale of priorities is important to keeping focused on the right goals in life. Working toward achieving what will ultimately be a less than satisfying goal makes no sense.

This is why it is important that we know what we are searching for in life. We need to think about not only what we want today but also what we might want tomorrow. We need to understand where we are headed in life and how to know if we are going in the right direction or need a different life strategy to be satisfied and happy in life.

Life Strategy Questions

Fill in the blank as it relates to your life: "If only I could _____, everything would be great then."

- How could filling in this blank make any significant difference in your life?
- Do you really believe that this is true?
- What are some Reality Checks in your life?
- How well are you facing these Reality Checks?
- How can thinking "politically" help you in your life?
- What things are put on "hold" that are interfering with your progress towards your goals in life? How can you "release" or eliminate these holds?
- What is your "risk tolerance" in life?
- How do your priorities change in life?

Endpoints

You may never reach all your goals in life but just as the stars, they serve to guide you along your journey. Not reaching your goals may not always be a bad thing. Sometimes you discover even more important and meaningful things along the way that you never would have discovered otherwise. Keep in mind that there may be more than one way to reach your destinations and goals. Multiple paths may lead to your happiness and contentment in life.

Having a Winning Life Strategy of your own is perhaps the most important thing you can do for yourself. Your Life Strategy should help you find satisfaction in just about any situation in which you find yourself. It can help determine your happiness not only today but in the future as well. The great

Negotiating Life Strategies

thing about your life strategy is that you can negotiate it for yourself. You sit on both sides of the table and negotiate your life strategy with yourself. Ultimately, there is no way you can lose in this negotiation. You win either way!

Winning Either Way

About the Author

Peter R. Garber is the accomplished author of over 40 books and articles on a variety of workplace topics including training, customer service, supervisory development, human resources, leadership and management. He has worked as a Human Resources Professional for over 25 years in a variety of roles and positions, and is considered an expert in this field.

He lives in Wexford, Pennsylvania, U.S.A.

Winning Either Way

Did you like this book?

If you enjoyed this book, you will find more interesting books at

www.MMPubs.com

Please take the time to let us know how you liked this book. Even short reviews of 2-3 sentences can be helpful and may be used in our marketing materials. If you take the time to post a review for this book on Amazon.com, let us know when the review is posted and you will receive a free audiobook or ebook from our catalog. Simply email the link to the review once it is live on Amazon.com, your name, and your mailing address -- send the email to orders@mmpubs.com with the subject line "Book Review Posted on Amazon."

If you have questions about this book, our customer loyalty program, or our review rewards program, please contact us at info@mmpubs.com.

Your Business Publisher since 1988.

Want to Get Ahead in Your Career?

Do you find yourself challenged by office politics, bad things happening to good careers, dealing with the "big cheeses" at work, the need for effective networking skills, and keeping good working relation-ships with coworkers and bosses?

Winning the Rat Race at Work is a unique book that provides you with case studies, interactive exercises, self-assessments, strategies, evaluations, and models for overcoming these workplace challenges. The book illustrates the stages of a career and the career choices that determine your future, empowering you to make positive changes.

Written by Peter R. Garber, the author of *100 Ways to Get on the Wrong Side of Your Boss*, this book is a must read for anyone interested in getting ahead in his or her career. You will want to keep a copy in your top desk drawer for ready reference whenever you find yourself in a challenging predicament at work.

ISBN: 1-895186-68-4   (paperback)

Also available in ebook formats. Order from your local bookseller, Amazon.com, or directly from the publisher at

www.mmpubs.com/rats

Need More Help with the Politics at Work?

100 Ways To Get On The Wrong Side Of Your Boss (And Strategies to Prevent You from Getting There!) was written for anyone who has ever been frustrated by his or her working relationship with the boss—and who hasn't ever felt this way!

Bosses play a critically important role in your career success and getting on the wrong side of this important individual in your working life is not a good thing. Each of these 100 Ways is designed to illustrate a particular problem that you may encounter when dealing with your boss and then an effective strategy to prevent this problem from reoccurring. You will learn how to deal more effectively with your boss in this fun and practical book filled with invaluable advice that can be utilized every day at work.

Written by Peter R. Garber, the author of *Winning the Rat Race at Work*, this book is a must read for anyone inter-ested in getting ahead. You will want to keep a copy in your top desk drawer for ready reference whenever you find yourself in a challenging predicament at work.

ISBN: 1-895186-98-6   (paperback)

Order from your local bookseller, Amazon.com, or directly from the publisher at **www.InTroubleAtWork.com**

The Elusive Lean Enterprise: Why Companies Struggle to Get the Full Benefits from Lean

In today's fast-paced and volatile business environment, customers are demanding increased flexibility and lower cost, and companies must operate in a waste-free environment to maintain a competitive edge and grow margins. Lean Enterprise is the process that companies are adopting to provide superior customer service and improve bottom line performance.

Are you contemplating Lean Enterprise for your manufacturing or office facility? Are you already implementing Lean, but dissatisfied with the speed of change? Do your employees think that Lean is just the new flavor of the month? Are you being forced to go Lean by your customers? This book is designed to help guide you through the Lean transformation and avoid the pitfalls. Find out why many companies are failing to live up to the promise of Lean, and why there may be alternatives to outsourcing or going offshore.

ISBN: 1-897326-64-5   (paperback)
ISBN: 1-897326-65-3   (hardcover)
ISBN: 1-897326-66-1   (Adobe PDF ebook)

Order from your local bookseller, Amazon.com, or directly from the publisher at **www.mmpubs.com**

Networking *for* Results
THE POWER OF PERSONAL CONTACT

In partnership with Michael J. Hughes, *The* Networking Guru, Multi-Media Publications Inc. has released a new series of books, ebooks, and audio books designed for business and sales professionals who want to get the most out of their networking events and help their career development.

Networking refers to the concept that each of us has a group or "network" of friends, associates and contacts as part of our on-going human activity that we can use to achieve certain objectives.

The *Networking for Results* series of books, audiobooks, and DVDs shows us how to think about networking strategically, and gives us step-by-step techniques for helping ourselves and those around us achieve our goals. By following these best practices, we can greatly improve our personal networking effectiveness.

Visit **www.Networking-for-Results.com** for information on specific products in this series, to read free articles on networking skills, or to sign up for a free networking tips newsletter. Products are available from most book, ebook, and audiobook retailers, or directly from the publisher at **www.mmpubs.com**.

Lessons from the Ranch for Today's Business Manager

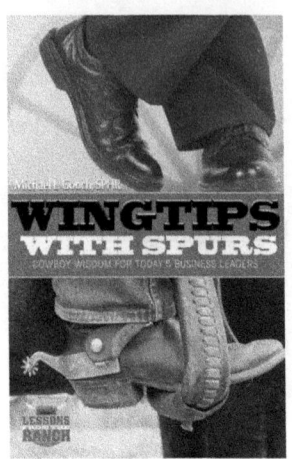

The lure of the open plain, boots, chaps and cowboy hats makes us think of a different and better way of life. The cowboy code of honor is an image that is alive and well in our hearts and minds, and its wisdom is timeless.

Using ranch based stories, author Michael Gooch, a ranch owner, tells us how to apply cowboy wisdom to our everyday management challenges. Serving up straight forward, practical advice, the book deals with issues of dealing with conflict, strategic thinking, ethics, having fun at work, hiring and firing, building strong teams, and knowing when to run from trouble.

A unique (and fun!) approach to management training, Wingtips with Spurs is a must read whether you are new to management or a grizzled veteran.

ISBN: 1-897326-88-2   (paperback)

Also available in ebook formats. Order from your local bookseller, Amazon.com, or directly from the publisher at **www.mmpubs.com**

Are People Finding Your Meetings Unproductive and Boring?

Turn ordinary discussions into focused, energetic sessions that produce positive results. If you are a meeting leader or a participant who is looking for ways to get more out of every meeting you lead or attend, then this book is for you. It's filled with practical tips and techniques to help you improve your meetings.

You'll learn to spot the common problems and complaints that spell meeting disaster, how people who are game players can effect your meeting, fool-proof methods to motivate and inspire, and templates that show you how to achieve results. Learn to cope with annoying meeting situations, including problematic participants, and run focused, productive meetings.

ISBN: 1-897326-15-7   (paperback)

Also available in other ebook formats. Order from your local bookseller, Amazon.com, or directly from the publisher at **www.mmpubs.com**

www.ingramcontent.com/pod-product-compliance
Lightning Source LLC
Chambersburg PA
CBHW071425160426
43195CB00013B/1818